Korean Royal Palace

Gyeongbokgung

Korean Royal Palace : Gyeongbokgung

Text · Illustration : Yi Hyang-woo
Translation : Won Hyeon-suk, Yi Choonsun
Supervision : Na Gak-sun, Terry S. Kim
Photograph : Heo Kyong-hee, Yi Hyang-woo

Published : April 7, 2014
Third edition : June 15, 2016
Published by : INMUNWALK Publishing Co.
Publisher : Heo Kyong-hee

Address : 445-4, Hoedong-gil, Paju-si, Gyeonggi-do, Korea, 10881
E-mail : inmunwalk@naver.com
Telephone No. : 82-31-949-9792
Facsimile No. : 82-31-949-9793
Registration of Publishing : September 1, 2009

ISBN 978-89-98259-10-5   03910

This book has been funded to be translated by Publication Industry Promotion Agency of Korea.

This book's CIP of the National library of Korea is able to use through 'http://seoji.nl.go.kr' and 'http://www.nl.go.kr/kolisnet'. (CIP No.: CIP2014009783)

Korean Royal Palace
Gyeongbokgung

Text · Illustration   Yi Hyang – woo
Translation   Won Hyeon – suk, Yi Choonsun
Supervision   Na Gak – sun, Terry S. Kim

INMUNWALK

Contents

1

A Road to
Gwanghwamun Gate

On the day I took a visit to Gyeongbokgung,
I saw a butterfly flying into the palace wall along with me······

Shall We Take a Stroll to Gyeongbokgung Palace?

Would you like to read the tales on the Joseon people in Korea under the elegantly curved roof and upon the gorgeously flower-patterned brick walls of Gyeongbokgung (景福宮) Palace? Please imagine yourself being in the midst of the Jamidang Hall site in one spring day and seeing an apricot tree's white petals fluttering all over. Moreover, what would be better than strolling the loft of Gyeonghoeru Pavilion, listening to court music *Sujecheon* (wind music ensembles) wafted on a breeze, and looking over a willow being highly elated on high summer day's *pungryu* (風流, elegant culture) at leisure?

At the place where long ago the court trainees with their hair braided in two locks brushed by, smiling at each other and walking softly on a long corridor building, we become a moonlight lingering at Hamwolji Pond of Amisan Mound within the walls of Gyotaejeon Hall and get intoxicated by the aroma of the autumn chrysanthemum.

In winter when the scent of lotus flowers under Chwihyanggyo Bridge is evanescing, I wish to be white snow

The road to the Hyangwonjeong Pavilion in Gyeongbokgung Palace

accumulated on trees at Hyangwonjeong Pavilion. And when the early spring comes again with the scent of apricot trees suffusing all over, we will be hearing young bird's clear sounds of chirping and windy sounds arising from the bamboo forest, won't we?

Gyeongbokgung Palace is the first-built palace of the Joseon Dynasty and the last-rebuilt artwork by Regent Heungseon, Yi Ha-eung, biological father of King Gojong, embodying Joseon's architectural tradition.

There are many ways to look around Gyeongbokgung. You

can look into cultural and historical transitions in detail from various angles, or you will just spend time enjoying a stroll at leisure. It would be great to be guided by an expert in palace, but it could be uncomfortable to be with somebody all along. Let me give you a helpful tip as the one who has visited the palace; strolling alone the palace without getting any interruption from someone else has a charm of its own.

Every time I visit the palace, I would like to follow as my heart leads. With one or more casual visits, you may feel the time at the palace seems standstill. When you take trips to palaces frequently enough, you will realize how awesome and how different they look at each time of your visit. Every season they do reveal different looks. Even the different look of the sky lets you enjoy different features of the palace. On rainy days, the court is filled with strong impression due to desolation; still I enjoy the melancholy. That is because I would like to taste an atmosphere of the old days people lived there, to share their joys and sorrows through communion, and to be included into their lives.

However, this relaxing time can only be secured with the perspective from which you find out and appreciate something there. That is because in order to invite them out, you need to get much closer to those who concealed themselves behind

Gyeongbokgung Palce seen from Gwanghwamun Gate

history. This book does not try any profound historical interpretations nor delve into deep philosophical concepts. I just hope you will hold the Joseon people and their space in common and feel them from the place you are now in. I know you have longed for a calm and easy walk around the palace at your leisure. You deserve the book teeming with my heartful paintings.

Gwanghwamun Plaza seen from the second floor of Gwanghwamun Gate

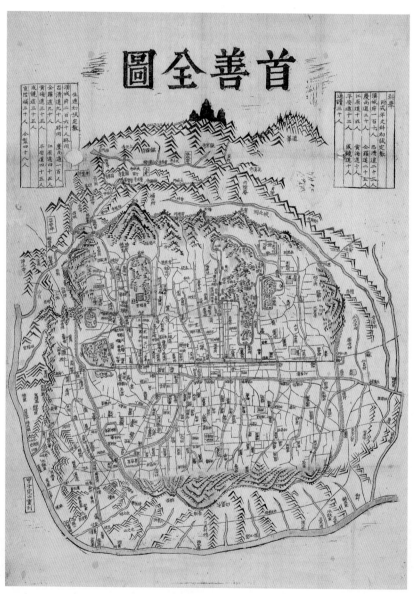

Suseonjeondo, the Map of 'Hanyang (current Seoul)'

14

Joseon Goes Down to the New History

The Joseon (朝鮮) Dynasty began to make new 500-year-long history on July 17, 1392 when King Taejo, Yi Seong-gye, ascended the throne at Suchanggung Palace in Gaegyeong (currently called Gaeseong, located in North Korea). Before long after he founded the dynasty, he projected to relocate the seat of government to a fresh location in a bid to stay away from invested interests of Gaegyeong, which had been the capital of the former Goryeo (高麗) Dynasty for 500 years. The king selected Hanyang (old name of Seoul) as a new capital in August 1394 and installed an office in charge of building the palace in the capital in September. Immediately after he determined where to build Jongmyo Shrine, State Altars, and Palace, he resolutely carried out historic relocation of the capital city on October 25, 1392. It is safe to say that all were intended politically to regain public trust, which had been alienated from the new government due to its dynastic revolution.

'Hanyang' picked as the new capital of the Joseon Dynasty is in the form of the large basin along the Han River. The new

The map of 'Hanyang Fortress Wall' during the Joseon Dynasty

capital is located in the center of the Korean peninsula, with Mt. Samgak (current Mt. Bukhan) and Mt. Gwanak facing each other and surrounding the city with the Han River in between. Mt. Samgak belongs to the northern mountain range stretching from the ✿ Baekdu-daegan Mountain System, whereas Mt. Gwanak is part of the southern one ranging from the same Baekdu-daegan Mountain System.

Hanyang was equipped with so many geographical advantages. The city was surrounded with ✿ the four inner mountains and ✿ the four outer ones, which furnished the capital with favorable terrain against foreign invaders. The inner

16

waterway called Cheonggyecheon stream joined the outer waterway, the Han River and then ran to the West Sea, which provided the city with convenient water-transportation. In other words, when it comes to geographical conditions, Hanyang as the capital of the fledgling dynasty was situated at a strategic key hub of politics, economy, traffic, and defense and blessed with a great natural boon.

✿ **Baekdu-daegan**: The Baekdu-daegan Mountain System means huge mountain peaks stretching from Mt. Baekdu. The Mountain System consists of high mountain peaks ranging from Mt. Baekdu in North Korea to Mt. Jiri in South Korea. The total length of it is 1,625 kilometers including the South Korean section covering 690 kilometers. Dubbed as the Spinal Ridge of Korea, the Baekdu-daegan has formed a dividing line of the province, language, and customs.

✿ **The four outer mountains**: Mt. Samgak (current Mt. Bukhan), Mt. Acha, Mt. Gwanak, Mt. Deogyang

✿ **The four inner mountains**: Mt. Baegak (current Mt. Bugak), Mt. Tarak (current Mt. Naksan), Mt. Mongmyeok (current Mt. Namsan), Mt. Inwang

The Newly Built Palace is Named 'Gyeongbok'

Gyeongbokgung Palace is the earliest one out of five palaces constructed in Hanyang by the Joseon Dynasty. The palace is nestled with Mt. Bugak at the back. Mt. Bugak was the main guardian mountain of Hanyang. To the west is seen Mt. Inwang. Down to the two mountains stands Gyeongbokgung facing the south south-east (SSE).

A view of Gyeongbokgung buildings standing along the north-south axis

The layout of the palace buildings follows strict principles of ideal palatial designs: the main buildings stand along the straight north-south axis, and they are arranged in symmetric pattern. Construction of Gyeongbokgung Palace was the pet project of the Joseon Dynasty, which made every effort to manifest architecturally their governing ideology of Neo-Confucinism.

'Gyeongbok' means 'Resplendent Happiness' and was named by Jeong Do-jeon (scholar official of early Joseon) under King Taejo's order. It comes from *Book of Odes*(詩經): "I am already intoxicated by alcohol and my stomach is full of moral virtue. May your Lordship enjoy 10,000 resplendent happiness." The passage is an eulogy on the new state with implication that the king and his descendants will enjoy the blessing of peace for 10,000 years, and that his benevolent governance will bring joy to the people.

The view of Heungnyemun and Mt. Bugak is beyond comparison
when you see them through the middle arch
with Red Phoenixes drawn on.

Five Palaces and Dual Palace System

What was the palace, '*gunggwol*,' like? '*Gung*' means buildings where king, king's family, court ladies and eunuches lived, and '*gwol*' refers to the walls surrounding the palace and watchtowers placed on both sides of the gate.

Joseon palaces followed the principles of ideal palatial design dictated by *Artificer's Record* (考工記) in the *Rites of Zhou* (周禮), an ancient Chinese document about urban planning and palace construction. The Joseon Dynasty adopted Neo-Confucianism as its ruling philosophy, thus the dynasty accepted the palace construction systems of the Zhou Dynasty (周朝), which was regarded as an ideal state devoted to acting upon Confucian monarchy. However, back in the Joseon Dynasty these principles served as just recommended standards rather than something that should not be broken. The city planners of Joseon considered harmony with the surrounding nature to be more crucial than manmade rules, and they applied the principles reasonably.

King Taejo (r. 1392~1398), the founder of the Joseon Dynasty, ascended the throne in Gaegyeong in 1392, moved the seat of

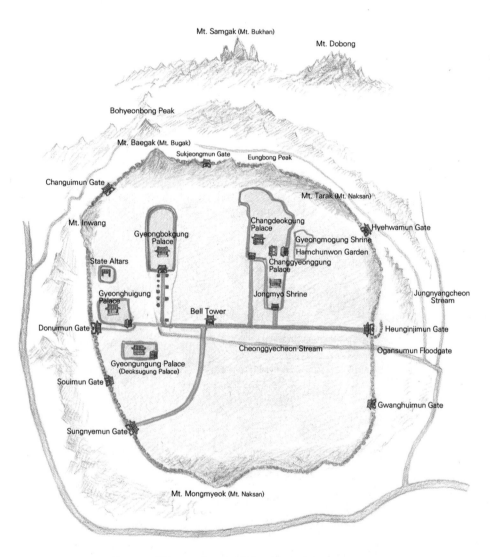

The map of 'Hanyang Fortress Wall' embracing the five palaces

government to Hanyang in 1394, and the next year constructed Gyeongbokgung Palace, Jongmyo Shrine, and State Altars. The palace was flanked by two important facilities: Jongmyo Shrine to the east and State Altars to the west. Jongmyo Shrine enshrines the spirit tablets of kings and queens, and ancestral rites are held there even now. State Altars dedicated to gods of land and grain was for praying for peace and prosperity of the dynasty. The primary palace of the Joseon Dynasty was Gyeongbokgung. It was the first-built royal residence that King Taejo set up right after he founded the dynasty in Gaegyeong and relocated the capital in order to find his own way away from established political clout.

Before long, the fledgling kingdom was drawn to chaos just like any other young dynasty. In the wake of the bloody rebellion (called ✿ the First Strife of Princes) initiated by Yi Bang-won (King Taejo's fifth son, the later Taejong), King Taejo (the founder) abdicated the throne and crowned his second son Yi Bang-gwa (later King Jeongjong) as the new leader. The first thing King Jeongjong (r. 1398~1400) did was to relocate the capital to Gaegyeong under the pretext of visiting the tomb of his mother, Queen Sinui. After that, Yi Bang-won retaining real power successfully defeated his fourth brother's forces (known as ✿ the second Strife of Princes) and was named as crown prince. He was in complete control of the court, patching up relations with his disgruntled father and soon assuming the throne as the third king, Taejong (r. 1400~1418).

King Taejong following his father's will pushed for relocation to Hanyang even if it was bitterly opposed by some officials. King Taejong returned to Hanyang, and he had the deserted Gyeongbokgung repaired and a new residence constructed on Hyanggyodong as a secondary palace. He always resided at the secondary palace named Changdeokgung and shunned

✿ **The First Strife of Princes:** King Taejo had eight sons; six sons with his first lawful wife Queen Sinui and two sons with his second lawful wife Queen Sindeok. The king appointed his eighth son Bang-seok as crown prince since the king wanted to appease Queen Sindeok. Bang-seok was the son between King Taejo and Queen Sindeok. Then frustrated Bang-won (the fifth son of King Taejo, a stepson of Queen Sindeok) staged a bloody strife, killing his two half brothers. As a result, Jeong Do-jeon and his followers were all executed because Bang-won and Jeong Do-jeon were bitter rivals. Bang-gwa (the second son of Taejo and Queen Sinui, later King Jeongjong) was installed as crown prince.

✿ **The Second Strife of Princes:** Bang-gan (the fourth son of King Taejo) initiated a rebellion due to his ambition to be a successor to the throne, failed to defeat his younger brother Bang-won, and ended up being exiled. After that, King Jeongjong nominated Bang-won as crown prince and finally abdicated the throne to him in November 1400. Two days later, Bang-won ascended the throne at Suchanggung palace.

Gyeongbokgung. It is assumed that King Taejong avoided Gyeongbokgung as it had been tainted by bloody struggle of killing Jeong Do-jeon, his arch political rival and his two half brothers. Gyeongbokgung had been regarded as the primary palace since the construction in 1395 and Changdeokgung built in 1405 was deemed the secondary palace.

It was King Sejong (r. 1418~1450) that furnished Gyeongbokgung with palatial scale as the primary royal residence. After he ascended the throne at Geunjeongjeon Hall, he restored, remodelled and added so many structures during his reign. Later on, King Seongjong got another residence constructed next to Changdeokgung and named it Changgyeonggung Palace. Gyeongbokgung served the primary palace, and Changdeokgung and Changgyeonggung were taken upon as the secondary palace. It was from King Sejong's reign to King Seongjong's reign that the palatial system was provided with its framework and formality.

Currently there still remain five palaces which served as primary or secondary palaces: Gyeongbokgung also called as Northern Palace, Changdeokgung and Changgyeonggung nicknamed Eastern Palaces, Gyeonghuigung also known as Western Palace, and Gyeongungung (later Deoksugung) otherwise known as Western Residence. All these five palaces did not simultaneously occupied by royals, but they were taken up one after another depending on the circumstances with being shut down or reconstructed every now and then.

Managing policy of the Joseon palaces was based on dual palace system: the primary and the secondary palaces. The Joseon kings resided in either the primary or the secondary palace alternately. The primary one was the core residence assigned for governing, and the secondary was extra one to move to as numerous occasions demanded. Not only political situations but also outbreak of diseases and king's personal needs were included in these occasions.

Restoration of Gyeongbokgung Palace and Japanese Annexation

The managing system of the Joseon royal palace took a huge turn when Japan invaded Korea in 1592. During the Japanese invasion (also known as Imjin Japanese Invasion), all the palace buildings were completely burnt down. When King Seonjo returned to the recaptured Hanyang from the shelter north of the capital in 1593, he had no choice but to temporarily reside in his relative's mansion, where he passed away 15 years later (1608). After the war, Dethroned King Gwanghaegun intended to rebuild the primary palace, Gyeongbokgung. However, he came to bend an ear to some fortunetellers, rebuilt Changdeokgung and Changgyeonggung Palaces first, and constructed a new Gyeongdeokgung Palace (later became Gyeonghuigung Palace).

Dethroned King Gwanghaegun had so insecure footing as a king that he condemned Prince Yeongchang, his half brother, in exile to Ganghwa Island and later murdered him. Moreover, he even incarcerated Queen Dowager Inmok, his step mother, in Gyeongungung (also known as Western Royal Residence). Dethroned King Gwanghaegun himself was reluctant to move to Changdeokgung for some time. Belatedly in 1615, the king began to reside in Changdeokgung. Also, he compelled the nation to construct a new palace called Gyeongdeokgung, only to be deposed by a coup in the following year.

Dual palace System under which 'Eastern Palaces' of Changdeokgung and Changgyeonggung served as the primary palace and 'Western Palace' of Gyeoghuigung as the secondary was the post-war management pattern of the Joseon palaces. Since then, this dual system had been employed for some 270 years until Gyeongbokgung was eventually reconstructed. In other words, Gyeongbokgung had been deserted in ruins for those long years.

Right after King Gojong succeeded the throne, a grand scale reconstruction of Gyeongbokgung started under the decree of Queen Dowager Jo (also known as Queen Sinjeong) with Regent Heungseon, the biological father of King Gojong taking the initiative.

According to *King Gojong's Annals*, Queen Dowager Jo issued a decree to entrust Regent Heungseon with a daunting task of palace reconstruction. Since the Japanese invasion ravaged Gyeongbokgung, successive kings had wished for reconstruction of Gyeongbokgung, the primary palace. Various circumstances, though, stopped them from carrying out the engineering project.

The grand construction project was on the point of getting started to assure the nation of royal authority and its authentic legitimacy. It is needless to say that so many people complained about being imposed too heavy taxation and excessive public service. Regent Heungseon initiated the palace construction and came to get a firm grip on the whole court behind the scenes. He was pushing forward with the reconstruction of the palace, a dynastic symbol, aiming for showing off supreme royal authority across the country and rejecting foreign powers.

Finally, rebuilding the palace in the greatest scale ever was

A view of Gwanghwamun equipped with the stone platform (The National Museum of Korea collection). It is presumed to have been taken away before Gwanghwamun was relocated, right after the ground-breaking of the Japanese Government-General building started.

completed in 1868, the fifth year of King Gojong's reign. With royal family including the king moving into Gyeongbokgung, the palace regained the status of the primary palace. Afterwards, the 12-year-old king grew up to pull himself out of his father's influence, constructed Geoncheonggung Palace behind Hyangwonjeong Pavilion, and started to rule the nation on his own.

However, Joseon suffered from foreign interventions from the late 19th century. In 1884, Japan defeated the Qing Dynasty of China in the war called the Sino-Japanese War (1894~1895) and brutally assassinated Queen Myeongseong at her own residence in 1895. King Gojong could not help taking shelter to the Russian Legation for fear of his life and his crown prince's. Consequently, the authentic resident owners of the palace had to leave their own residence, Gyeongbokgung, and the palace was on the verge of confronting with tragedy that it would lose all of its dignity and function as the primary palace.

During the one-year stay at the Russian Legation, he ordered to repair a detached palace called Gyeongungung and moved to that palace. Also, he promulgated the establishment of the Great Han Empire and assumed the title of emperor in 1897. Nevertheless, the new emperor dreaming of a true autonomy and independence of Korea was forced to abdicate the throne to

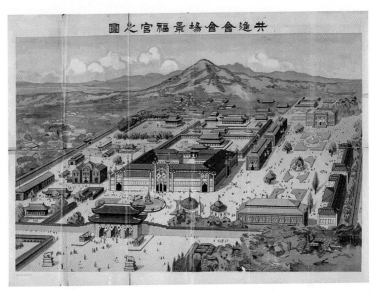

The painting map of Joseon Products Exhibition Site in Gyeongbokgung in commemoration of the fifth anniversary of Japanese annexation. The layout of the exhibition halls held in 1915 by Japan. From 1909 palace buildings were sold off to Japanese civilians, and a third of all the palace structures were torn down to host Joseon Products Exhibition in 1915.

his son Emperor Sunjong in 1907. Japan condemned Emperor Gojong with the incident involving dispatch of special envoys to the Hague. On August 27, 1907, Emperor Sunjong ascended the throne at Dondeokjeon Hall in Gyeongungung, and his father Emperor Gojong retired as an abdicated emperor and kept residing in Gyeongungung. At that time the name of the palace was changed to Deoksugung Palace.

On August 22, 1910, Joseon was forced to sign an annexation treaty and deprived of its sovereignty by Japan. Then Japanese authorities organized '✿ Joseon Products Exhibition' on the Gyeongbokgung ground in 1915 to commemorate the fifth anniversary of their colonial rule, and began to tear down palace buildings ruthlessly in order to build exhibition galleries and booths. From around 1915 Gyeongbokgung structures suffered drastic demolition, and about 1935 the palace ended up being turned into a public amusement park.

✿ **Joseon Products Exhibition**: The exhibition held in 1915 was politically projected to show off how much Korean economy grew under Japanese colonial rule. Exhibition halls were supposed to be built in the suburbs of the big city as exhibitions needed to secure large display space during a short period of time. On the contrary, Japanese colonialists held the exhibition on Gyeongbokgung ground, the very heart of the Joseon Dynasty. Demolishing a lot of palace buildings that Regent Heungseon had restored, they intended to humiliate royal authority. Also, hosting the exhibition in modernized Gyeongseong (old name of Seoul), they aimed to secure colonial authenticity by bragging that they had protected and promoted industrial development of dilapidated Joseon.

Gyeongbokgung Embodies
Confucian Ideals

To have a good grip on Joseon palaces, Gyeonbokgung should be the starting point. The palace means a lot not only as the first-built royal residence but also as the stern architectural framework representing ideal monarchy of Confucian society. From the layout to the naming of each and every structure, expressing their Confucian ideals occupied their first agenda. Now, shall we take a look at how they are arranged?

Geyongbokgung is seated with mountains at the back and streams in the front, in accordance with *pungsu* (風水, *fengshui* in Chinese) principles: to the back of the palace is Mt. Bugak (formerly Mt. Baegak), the main guardian mountain. To the south is Mt. Namsan, to the east is Mt. Tarak, and to the west is Mt. Inwang.

Palatial design of Gyeongbokgung follows the principles of 'front court and rear residence' and 'three gates and three courts.' The palace has government offices in the front, and private residences of the royal family and rear garden in the back Also, the area from the first gate, Gwanghwamun, to the third

33

gate, Geunjeongmun, is the outer court. The governing court is from Geunjeongmun to Sajeongjeon Hall, and the residential court is within the enclosure of Gangnyeongjeon and Gyotaejeon Halls.

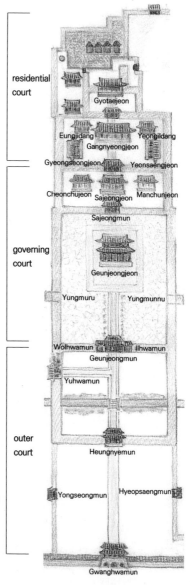

The layout of Gyeongbokgung Palace during King Gojong's reign

❖ *Bukgwol-dohyeong*, the *Map of the Northern Palace*

Bukgwol-dohyeong, the *Map of the Northern Palace* is a kind of blue print describing the layout of Gyeongbokgung buildings and its Rear Garden. Two editions have remained until now. The exact time of production is unknown, but they are presumed to have been made around 1907. Therefore, they are the priceless source as the survey map made in the Great Han Empire.

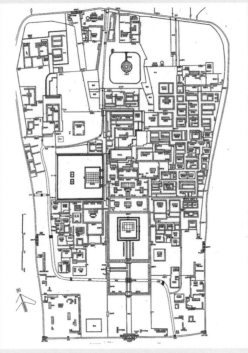

The Layout of the offices inside the palace on '*Bukgwol-dohyeong*,' the *Map of the Northern Palace*, made around 1907.

35

Four Gates and Watchtowers

Palatial walls are enclosing the palace compound, and there are large gates on four directions along the walls. A Hanyang history book called *Hangyeongjiryak* (a history book on old Seoul during the Joseon Dynasty) reads "Gyeongbokgung is located in the southern part of Gwangwangbang District in Hanyang. In the third year of

The Eastern Watchtower seen at the east end of the Gwanghwamun wall used to be part of the palace wall

Gwanghwamun and *haechi*

King Taejo's reign, palace walls were set up, and the walls contain gates on four directions: to the east Geonchunmun, to the south Gwanghwamun, to the west Yeongchumun, and to the north Sinmumun."

Gwanghwamun Gate

Gwanghwamun (光化門) is the main and south gate of Gyeongbokgung Palace. At first, it was just called 'Noon Gate' or 'Main Gate.' During King Sejong's reign, it began to be officially called 'Gwanghwamun Gate.' The name of 'Gwanghwa (光化)' means the brilliance of the king shines on the whole country

The west end of the Gwanghwamun wall used to have the Western Watchtower. You can only see the monument on the site.

and all the people. It has three arched entrances, and the middle entrance has Red Phoenixes painted on the ceiling. That is because Red Phoenix is a mythological animal in charge of the south as one of the Four Directional Guardians in the Chinese constellations. The eastern arch has Black Tortoises, and the western one has Qilins.

Gwanghwamun is the largest in size and the most magnificent in style, indicating that

The monument on the site of the Western Watchtower

The Eastern Watchtower

it is the main gate of the main palace of the Joseon Dynasty. The middle arch was for the king only, while the east and the west ones were for civil officials and military officials respectively.

At the ends of the Gwanghwamun walls, there used to be Eastern and Western Watchtowers. The main gates of the palace were supposed to secure watchtowers connected to the palace walls, but Gwanghwamun was the only main gate which was equipped with watchtowers. Also, there used to be lots of office buildings lining up in front of Gwanghwamun. These office buildings formed '✿ Street of Six Ministries (Yukjo-geori),' and the

During Japanese rule, the Eastern Watchtower was connected with the palace walls (The National Museum of Korea collection).

street was the main axis for politics and administration of the dynasty. Coming in touch with the street, a commercial town called '✿ Unjongga Street' was located. It manifests that Gwanghwamun meant a lot as a stately and dignified symbol of the Joseon palace by being seated in the center of political and commercial arenas.

Two watchtowers at the east and the west ends of the Gwanghwamun walls were damaged a lot as the palace compound got reduced, and the surrounding roads got expanded. The Eastern Watchtower ended up standing alone in the middle of the street, detached from the palace walls. What makes matters worse, the Western Watchtower was gone without a trace. In September 1923, Japanese authorities built tram car rails leading to Hyojadong Village and tore down the walls at the south-western corner of the palace. The tower is presumed to have been broken down along with the parts of the wall at that time.

The Eastern Watchtower was a pavilion standing at the south-eastern corner of the palace walls. Currently, the tower is standing all by itself in the middle of the street, which makes the tower awkward and out of the place. Even the cars moving on the street seem to be turning cold shoulders to the tower. Furthermore, most people do not care why such a structure should be there causing them too much trouble. Actually, it has remained so long where it was initially supposed to be. However,

✿ **Street of Six Ministries (Yukjo-geori)**: The name was derived from the offices of the six ministries lined up along both sides of the street. It is currently called Sejongno Street. Back in the Joseon Dynasty, the street served as the major thoroughfare running straight in front of Gwanghwamun, the main gate of Gyeongbokgung.

✿ **Unjongga Street**: 'Unjong (雲従)' means people rushing in like clouds. Unjongga refers to the current Jongno Street. Back then, the Unjongga neighborhood was a commercial area crowded with a large number of stores and shoppers

Geonchunmun, the east gate of Gyeongbokgung

the tower looks wrongly seated even if it has been rightly standing all the while. The palace wall was pulled way back from its original position, and the Eastern Watchtower ended up being such a nuisance. Like this, sometimes people put the cart before the horse in our world.

Geonchunmun Gate

'Geonchun (建春)' means founding spring. Geonchunmun (建春門) is the east gate of Gyeongbokgung. The direction of the east represents spring, and the east gate was named after spring. Also,

The wall is connecting Geonchunmun Gate and the Eastern Watchtower (The National Museum of Korea collection).

the ceiling of the gate has Blue Dragons, a guardian animal for the east. The gate was frequently used by royal family members and court ladies because the area inside the gate was used for living quarters including the crown prince's residence.

Across the street from Geonchunmun, there used to be the Office of Royal Pedigree. The office was in charge of the male and female descendants of Joseon Royal clan. It served to supervise the princes and censure the royal family of their misconduct.

Spring is in full bloom over the Geonchunmun wall.

The *Annals of King Sejong* says about Prince Sunpyeong (Yi
Gun-saeng, ?~1456). The lives of royal family members were not
always as happy and carefree as expected.

According to the fourth article in *King Sejong's Annals* on July
12, 1428, in the 10th year of King Sejong's reign, King Sejong
established the '*Jonghak* (宗學, prime disciplinary institute)' and had
royal kin including the princes attend the *Jonghak*.

❖ Prince Sunpyeong's story

King Sejong initiated the *Jonghak* and educated sons of the royal clan including the princes. During King Sejong's reign, the royal family members were banned from getting public posts, and they were likely to spend their days in low spirits with no effort into academic research. King Sejong was concerned that those members would get negligent in their disciplines, and that ignorant members would get shunned by people. Thus, he sometimes tested the royal members and rewarded successful members with some land. Still, it needs some aptitude for learning to catch up with others. Some royal relatives could not even write their own names. That brought erudite King Sejong into so much shame in front of his officials. Faculty members educating royal relatives were the greatest scholars nationwide. However, people need solid motivation in order to achieve something. They did not see any realistic returns for hardwork into academic research. They were quite well aware that they could not apply for the state examination and get promoted to higher positions.

Yi Gun-saeng was the illegitimate child of King Jeongjong. He was a son born of a concubine, Lady Gi, and was conferred to the title of Prince Sunpyeong in 1417 (the 17th year of King Taejong's reign). He remained utterly illiterate even when he reached over 40 years old. He was ordered to attend the *Jonghak* and to study *Book of Filial Duty* (孝經) for the first time. The tutor taught the first seven characters in the title of the first chapter. He could not read them at all. He said, "Now I am so old and slow-witted that I am fully satisfied with just two beginning characters in the title, 開宗." Then, he never stopped reciting the two characters even on the horseback. Also, he said to his servants, "You should remember these two characters and let me know them just in case I get stuck."

Prince Sunpyeong abhorred attending the *Jonghak* and was always so much worried that he might be humiliated in spite of his old age. Finally at his deathbed, he left a will to his family, "Even though I do care about death since life and death is of great concern, I feel greatly amused at departing from the *Jonghak*." In all ages, students will suffer. Prince Sunpyeong passed away in August 1456.

Yeongchumun Gate

Yeongchumun (迎秋門) is the west gate of Gyeongbokgung Palace and forms a pair with Geonchunmun Gate in the east. 'Yeongchu (迎秋)' means welcoming autumn. In accordance with the concept of 'Five Elements (fire, water, wood, metal and earth),' west corresponds to autumn, thus

The Yeongchumun wall falling down by shaking of trams (The National Museum of Korea collection)

the west gate was named 'welcoming autumn.' The gate has White Tigers painted on its ceiling since White Tigers are the guardian in charge of the west. It was mostly used by the officials of the Royal Secretariat.

This gate also went through sufferings. In 1926, the western wall of Gyeongbokgung collapsed due to shaking of trams which were carrying construction materials for the Japanese Government-General building. Japanese authorities removed the upper story of the gate and backed down Yeongchumun wall. The current gate was restored with reinforced concrete in 1975, 50 meters north of the original site.

46

Yeonghchumun, the west gate of Gyeongbokgung

Autumn foliage on Hyojaro Street along the Yeongchumun wall

Sinmumun Gate

Sinmumun (神武門) seated west of the Jibokjae Hall is the north gate of Gyeongbokgung. It was named 'Sinmumun' in the 6th year of King Seongjong's reign (1475). The gate is as large as Geonchunmun in size, and Black Tortoises (玄武), the guardian of the north, are painted on the ceiling.

Sinmumun, the north gate of Gyeongbokgung

'Sinmu (神武)' means marvelous military prowess.

Sinmumun located in the northwestern part of the palace was usually kept shut except when the king visited the Rear Garden. The neighboring area was rarely used, but it was where the covenant altar was built nearby. The king used Sinmumun to attend the ✿covenant ceremony with his officials. Also, King Yeongjo made frequent use of the gate when he traveled to Yuksanggung Shrine, which enshrined the spirit tablet of Lady Choe, his birth mother.

✿ **Covenant Ceremony**: The king would hold a ritual called the covenant ceremony by offering animal sacrifice and sharing the blood of the offerings with his meritorious retainers.

The inner part of Sinmumun Gate is the best spot to view Mt. Bugak.

Guardian animals on the ceilings of the four gates of Gyeongbokgung

Red Phoenixes of Gwanghwamun

Blue Dragons of Geonchunmun

White Tigers of Yeongchumun

Black Tortoises of Sinmumun

Starting from the Gwanghwamun Plaza

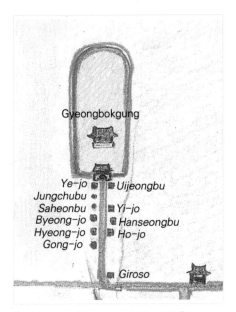

Gwanghwamun Plaza where Yukjo-geori Street was located back in the Joseon Dynasty

Would you please stop for a moment in the center of the Gwanhwamun Plaza and face Gwanhwamun Gate? I would like to guide you in Gyeongbokgung Palace tour planned just for you.

Back in the Joseon Dynasty, before entering Gyeongbokgung, Yukjo-geori (Street of Six Ministries) stood along both sides of Gwanghwamun: Yukjo-geori means the street where the government offices outside the palace were located. They include *Uijeongbu* (State council), *Yi-jo* (Ministry of Personnel), *Ho-jo* (Ministry of Taxation), *Hanseongbu* (Seoul Metropolitan Government), and ✿ *Giroso* (Club of the Elders) on the east. On the west *Ye-jo* (Ministry of Rites), *Jungchubu* (Office of Ministers-without-Portfolio), *Saheonbu* (Office of the Inspector-

51

General), *Byeong-jo* (Ministry of Military Affairs), *Hyeong-jo* (Ministry of Punishments), *Gong-jo* (Ministry of Public Works), and *Jangyewon* (Office of Servants). Currently, only the site of *Uijeongbu* is restored as a place for relaxation, and the other offices are roughly marked with stone milesone. With the passage of time, roads have got changed or broadened, but all the time their traces have remained. Likewise, the old Yukjo-geori has maintained the time-honored tradition of government office quarters, since the street is lined up with political arena, such as the Integrated Government Complex, the Ministry of Foreign Affairs, and the US Embassy. In addition, 'National Museum of Korean Contemporary History' is showcasing the flow of modern history on the street. Yukjo-geori is now named Sejongno Street, which joins Jongno Street that was called Unjongga Street back then.

✿ *Giroso* Office: It was established to treat courteously chief state ministers over the age 70 and seated at the east end of the Yukjo-geori, now in front of the Kyobo building. Joseon kings were also able to be inducted to the *Giroso* Office. King Taejo was inducted at the age of 60, King Sukjong at 59, and King Yeongjo at 51. King Gojong was born in 1852 and registered on the *Giroso* roster in 1902 at the age of 51, following the example of King Yeongjo.

Would you please stop for a moment in the center of
the Gwanghwamun Plaza and face Gwanghwamun?

Memorial Stele on Yukjo-geori

In front of the Kyobo building at the corner of Gwanghwamun rotary toward Jongno Street, you will meet the Memorial Stele erected to commemorate Emperor Gojong being inducted to *Giroso*. 'Memorial Stele dedicated to the 40th year of Emperor Gojong's enthronement' was built to celebrate the 40th anniversary of Emperor Gojong's coronation and his 51st

Memorial Stele and its front gate

Various Sculptures of the Memorial Stele

birthday. In 1902, the crown prince (later Emperor Sunjong) took the initiative in conferring the honorific title on Emperor Gojong and erecting the Memorial Stele.

You need to muster up your courage to take a close look at the carvings on its front gate. Actually, what you need more is not taking your courage, but shrugging off your shyness. That is because no one has interest in the fact that there are some carvings over there. Just taking a peep at the building will attract everyone's eyes.

Most of the people are standing there just waiting for the

Mansemun Gate with unusual patterns

traffic light to change green. Once in a while, you see some people demonstrating over microphones. If you take some pictures around the Memorial Stele, people may think you are up to something.

Carving skills expressed in stone animal statues along the railings of the double foundation look so excellent. When you look at them more closely, you will find the engraving ability is comparable to that on the stone platforms of Geunjeongjeon in Gyeongbokgung. You will be impressed by all-out efforts of the artisans.

Haechi Statues in Front of Gwanghwamun Gate

Shall we get much closer to Gwanghwamun now? You will find a pair of *haechi* statues sitting closer to both sides of the palace walls and guarding the gate. With their eyes glaring and their lips firmly closed, they look so scary as to deserve to be gate guards. However, who cares? The reality is *haechis* are just watching all day the endless waves of vehicles passing by

Haechi is strictly enforcing the law

Gwanghwamun.

It is said that *haechis* were placed at the palace since they were known to expel fires. Let us give it another thought, though. The initial position for *haechis* was both sides of the street in front of the old *Saheonbu* (Office of the Inspector-General), which was the representative law enforcement agency, discriminating the rights and wrongs of the public cases, monitoring official misconduct, and impeaching those who committed irregularities. The *haechi* served a symbol of the law, and *Saheonbu* officials used breast insignia embroidered with a *haechi* figure and wore a *haechi* headgear.

The *haechi*, also called *haetae*, is an imaginary creature appearing in a legend of ancient China. According to the old literature called *Record of Rarities of Odd Things* (異物志), the *haechi* with only one horn had such a fair and just character that it could distinguish the crooked from the straight. When the

Original place of *haechi* statues earmarked on the Gwanghwamun Plaza

Gwanhwamun and *haechi* (The National Museum of Korea collection). The photo shows the original place of the *haechi* statue is different from the current one. *Nodutdol* was in front of the *haechi* statue.

fightings occurred, the *haechi* was said to butt the guilty with its horn and bite the liars with its teeth. In the reign of Emperor Shun (舜皇帝) in Ancient China, there was a wise law enforcement official called Gao Yao (皐陶). He placed a *haechi* in front of the prison gate and picked out the guilty.

It is assumed that the original place of the *haechi* statues, which are now seated in front of Gwanghwamun, was way down the street between the Sejong Cultural Center and the Integrated Government Complex. They also served as the sign of dismounting from a horse. Photos taken in the 1890s show an L-shaped stone block in front of the *haechi* statues. It is '*nodutdol*,' a stepping stone used when getting off the horse. '*Nodutdol*' was a sign that anyone below the king must get off their horse or palanquin before taking a step into the palace since the stone was the starting point of the sacred arena of the king.

However, nowadays you do not have to get off your conveyance even if you notice *haechi* sitting closer to the palace wall. You can not only dash down the street before *haechi* in your car but also use 'king's entrance,' the middle arch of Gwanghwamun. Who cares? The dynasty already ended, and you are now living in the equal and democratic society with no kings. You do not have to look up Gyeongbokgung with reverence. Moreover, you are free as you do not need to be aware of that.

I feel so sorry about the totally indifferent *haechis* that lost their original position, righteous spirit, and essential function. They even remind me of a shadow of the fallen dynasty. Am I overreacting?

When you understand and approach the view of nature and significant philosophy of the Joseon people who created Gyeongbokgung, you will come to read their thoughts from a small lifeless rock and get back truly Korean things to your own heart.

Gwanghwamun Gate at night

At Gwanghwamun you can watch the grandiose and colorful
'Changing of Gates' Guards'

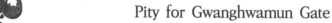

Gwanghwamun was erected in 1395 as the main gate of Gyeongbokgung Palace, destroyed by arson in the Japanese Invasion of Korea in 1592, and reconstructed by Regent Heungseon in the late Joseon Dynasty. From then on, the gate held out all the Joseon people screaming through the Japanese

Gyeongbokgung and its vicinity seen from Mt. Bugak in 1926 (The National Museum of Korea collection). The dome spire is distorted to the east and the axis of the Japanese Government-General building does not conform to the main axis of the Gyeongbokgung. The Japanese authorities seemed to rotate the main axis of the building 3.75 degrees clockwise so that the building could be facing the Japanese Shinto Temple located on Mt. Namsan.

occupation, and now it has become the pitiful but proud Korean history itself.

Major buildings of Gyeongbokgung Palace are seated along the same linear axis in the order of Gwanghwamun (The Main and South Gate), Heungnyemun (The Second Inner Gate), Geunjeongmun (The Third Inner Gate), Geunjeongjeon (The King's Throne Hall), Sajeongjeon (The Council Hall), Gangnyeongjeon (The King's Residence), Gyotaejoen (The Queen's Residence). In 1926, the Japanese colonial authorities completed the Japanese Government-General building in the palace compound and intended to completely tear down

The Japanese Government-General building seen over Geunjeongmun Gate

Gwanghwamun Gate was shifted to the north of Geonchunmun Gate (The National Museum of Korea collection)

Gwanghwamun because it was right in front of their colonial headquarters. Facing strong public opposition, they backed down and instead moved the building to the north of Geonchunmun (The East Gate) in September 1927, where the main gate of the National Folk Museum is currently located.

Gwanghwamun Gate was deprived of its function as the main palace entrance and expelled to the northeastern section of the palace. The gate took additional blow as it lost the wooden upper story due to the bombing during the Korean War and ended up with only the stone structure left. In 1968, during Park Chung-hee's presidency, the gate was restored as the main

64

palace entrance and moved back to the center of the south wall. However, the wall was relocated inward, 14.5 meters to the north, and the axis was also rotated toward the southeast of the original one.

Back then, the Korean government took over the Japanese Government-General building and they used it as the Capitol building of Korea. From the outset the building occupied the location different from the main axis of Gyeongbokgung. Under this condition, Gwanghwamun standing before the Capitol building had to be rotated 3.75 degrees and could not conform the layout of the palace buildings. Furthermore, the upper story was restored in reinforced concrete rather than wood. Consequently, they did not have to be worried that the gate would be burnt down by fire, but they lost the tradition of palace architecture. The restored gate did not meet the standard to be deserving of cultural property, tarnishing its true historical significance.

Fortunately, on August 15, 2010, Gwanghwamun unveiled its grandeur in its authentic seat after Gwanghwamun restoration project was completed. Originally Gwanghwamun was equipped with the stone platform. Unfortunately, the current traffic condition did not allow the stone platform to be fully restored and the *haechi* statues to get back to their original position.

Recently, as the Cultural Heritage Administration tried to change the name plaque of the gate again, Gwanghwamun came to be the issue of controversy, which gave a chance to reflect on the initial shape. However, I am well aware that the clumsy restoration will lead to another issue, and I am looking forward to the day the prudent historical researches will ensure the authentic restoration of cultural property.

With the finish of the restoration project of Gwanghwamun in 2010, you can walk directly to Gwanghwamun from the Gwanghwamun Plaza through the former Yukjo-geori (Street of Six Ministries, present Sejongno Street). Before the restoration, you had to use the crosswalk close to the Eastern Watchtower or the street ahead of Yeongchumun (The West Gate). Now, you enjoy proceeding to the palace, facing forward the facade of the gate with your heads up. The visual grandeur you come across in the center of the plaza makes lots of difference even though Yukjo-geori is gone.

The staircase leading to the upper story of Gwanghwamun

The door at the end of the staircase

The colorful inner brackets in the upper story of Gwanghwamun

The upper story of Gwanghwamun brightly shone by the sunlight

Nonetheless, there are not so many people who are concerned about the real role of Gangwhamun. No doubt the main entrance to Gyeongbokgung is Gwanghwamun. However, Heungnyemun Gate where you show your ticket serves as the practical entrance to Gyeongbokgung. You are likely to regard the Gwanghwamun compound as the large venue or the path for

67

Gyeongbokgung, the primary palace of the Joseon Dynasty still cherishes its brilliance.

enacting old ceremonies like 'Changing of the Gates' Guards.' Gwanghwamun, the main gate of Gyeongbokgung, is grand enough to demand your attention, though.

You can enjoy watching magnificent spectacle of 'Changing of the Gates' Guards' at the Gwanghwamun Plaza. Some tourists have fun taking pictures with gate guards wearing military uniforms of the Joseon Dynasty even before starting the palace tour. If you say you love the night view of Gwanghwamun more than that of the day, other people will agree with you, nodding their heads. Fabulous Gwanghwamun under the glaring lights sometimes made me feel that way, too.

❖ Yanagi Muneyoshi Speaks of Gwanghwamun Gate

"Gwanghwamun, Gwanghwamun, alas, your life is in a dire extremity. The memory that you existed in this world in the past is about to disappear into cold oblivion. What shall I do? I feel completely lost. It will not be long before merciless chisel and uncaring hammer start to destroy your body little by little. Lots of people will be heartbroken at the thought of this happening. Nevertheless, there is no one to be able to save you. Unfortunately, those who are capable of rescuing you do not feel sorry about you."

The above is part of the editorial written in September 1922 by Yanagi Muneyoshi (柳宗悦, 1889~1961), Japanese folk arts scholar. Its title was "For a Joseon Architecture Running into Danger of Disappearing", and it was contributed to a Japanese magazine in a bid to oppose the decision of the Japanese Governor-General in Korea to tear down Gwanghwamun. In May 1921, the Dong-A Daily News (Korean newspaper) ran a big photo of the gate and for the first time made a revelation to the plan to tear it down. The article said that by the time the new Government-General building was completed, Gwanghwamun would be pulled down by the Japanese Governor-General. Japanese authorities already made up their mind to demolish the gate since Gwanghwamun was a irreverent structure blocking their new Government-General building.

His text was issued when most of the local media hushed up the plan out of the fear for the Japanese Governor-General office, and had far-reaching repercussions among Koreans. The editorial whose title was "Alas, Gwanghwamun" was translated into Korean and ran in the Dong-A Daily news. However, it turned out that a large part of the handwritten manuscript of Yanagi Muneyoshi, who was a conscientious cultural activist in Japan, was not released because of the Japanese censorship.

Gwanghwamun with its wooden structure burned down and only the stone structure left during the Korean War

"Can you even imagine Japan would be annexed by Joseon, the palace in Japan would be ruined, and western-styled colonial building in large scale would be erected in its place if only Joseon prospered and Japan waned?"

"The world is excessive with contradictions. Those who are alive, will be held accountable for treason [when such a thing occurs]."

The two above sentences hidden to public due to the censorship help you to see how harsh Yanagi criticized Japanese authorities for their plot to demolish Gwanghwamun. Not only Yanagi but also Professor Ima Wajiro at Waseda University, who was recognized in Japan as an architect and art critic, pointed out it was unjust to tear down the gate. Public sentiment against the removal of the gate was mounting in Korea. From the outset, Japan had an ulterior motive to wipe out Korean identity and national spirit through removing Gwanghwamun and erecting their colonial building right before the primary palace, Gyeongbokgung.

Yet, they might have been quite well aware of Koreans' strong opposition to the gate removal and ended up moving the location, scrapping the removal plan. Then, in October 1923, two *haechi* statues serving as the gate guards on both sides of Gwanghwamun were taken away.

The Chosun Ilbo (Korean daily newspaper) ran on October 26, 1925, a mournful farewell article on Gwanghwamun whose title was "I Am Leaving." It was written in the form that Gwanghwamun spoke in its own mouth on how depressed and heartless Koreans were feeling on the verge of its being dismantled, with no one to appeal to. After all, on July 22, 1926, the fate of Joseon met its final end and all ancestors' spirits waking from the nether world were crying and wailing bitterly. The demolition of the gate began right away. Even though it was not the total destruction but just moving to the side of Geonchunmun, the gate would get its existence value fading away on leaving its original seat. After the removing operation was begun, the Dong-A Daily News ran an article on August 29, 1926, the title of which was "Gwanghwamun Breakup Set a Few Days Ago."

"…The relocation project of Gwanghwamun, the main gate of Gyeongbokgung, set the dismantlement started a few days ago. The Japanese Government-General paid Miyakawakumi Company 54,800 *won* for the project, and the construction is scheduled to be completed within a year…."

After that, Gwanghwamun relocated to the north of Geonchunmun had the wooden structure burned during the Korean War and only the stone masonry left.

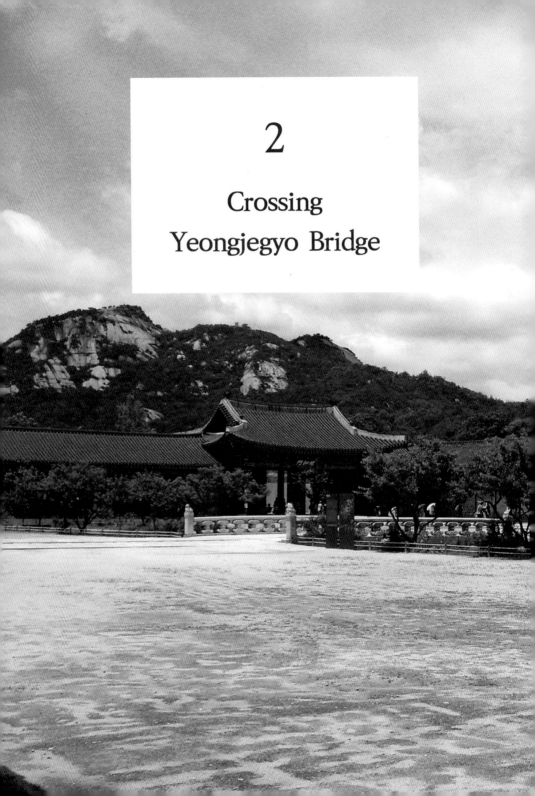

2

Crossing
Yeongjegyo Bridge

Would you like to look into Gyeongbokgung Palace through the middle arch of Gwanghwamun Gate?

Entering Heungnyemun Gate

Up to now, we have looked at the outside of Gwanghwamun Gate, the Street of Six Ministries, Yukjo-geori. Shall we now go into the palace through Heungnyemun(興禮門) Gate? Heungnyemun is the second south gate of Gyeongbokgung Palace. At first, it was called Hongnyemun (弘禮門), but during King Gojong's reign, it was changed to Heungnyemun. Using the character 'hong (弘),' the same character as Emperor Qianlong's name, Hong Li (弘曆),

Changing of the Gates' Guards ceremony is being performed in front of Heungnyemun Gate.

Dapdo and *haechi* placed on the staircase of Heungnyemun Gate.

in Qing Dynasty of China was considered improper.

Now, we can find the sculptures placed on the staircase of Heungnyemun which are conspicuously showing mythical animals, *haechi*, described in Record of *Rarities or Odd Things* (異物誌).

After we enter Heungnyemun, we can see Yuhwamun Gate across Yeongjegyo Bridge on the left. There were the offices inside the palace beyond Yuhwamun. At the space between Geunjeongmun Gate and Heungnyemeun Gate, the royal court held not only a regular audience but also conducted cross examination on felony and promulgated the king's messages. Therefore, government officials needed a gate which they could frequent without a hitch, and Yuhwamun played the role.

A small room on the right side of Yuhwamun is news reporting office, *Gibyeolcheong*. In the office, the clerks wrote

Yuhwamun Gate and Gibyeolcheong Office

about issues of the state affairs, which were handled by the Royal Secretariat, and distributed them every five days, and this was called 'news or *gibyeol*.' The news was distributed in the morning, so it was called 'the morning news or *jobo*.' The officials of government departments located on the Street of Six Ministries visited the news reporting office and copied down the news related to their offices; and to local governments, the news was sent through express messengers.

A dragon on a newel post of Yeongjegyo Bridge is grasping a *cintamani* and is guarding against its surrounding.

Yeongjegyo Bridge and Mythical Animals

After we enter Heungnyemun, we need to cross a stone
bridge over a small stream before we get to the core of the
palace. This is Yeongjegyo Bridge over Yeongjecheon Stream.
When we go to a Buddhist temple, we have to cross a stream to
purify our mind before entering Buddha's world. Just like a
temple, the stone bridge is there to calm ourselves down and to

Yeongjegyo Bridge with the spring blossoms

Stone beasts on top of Yeongjegyo Bridge left abandoned by Japanese imperialists during the occupation (The National Museum of Korea collection).

forbid outsiders from trespassing. The palace was a sacred area where the kings expanded politics, thus Yeongjegyo was a symbolic border that distinguished the king's area from the general public's. Moreover, Yeongjecheon Stream was made to flow from the west to the east as a propitious waterway based on a notion of auspicious *pungsu* (風水, *fengshui* in Chinese), of which landscape had a mountain in the back and a stream in the front. Under the bridge were constructed two arches, and on the bridge was set up three-lane road (三道), with the middle lane reserved for the king.

Cheollok is described as a mythical animal.

There are four stone beasts that are watching a waterway quite fiercely along the stone embankments of Yeongjecheon Stream. They are squatting down as if ready to jump into the water. They are guarding the palace from any bad energy coming through the waterway. In the *Record of Gyeongbokgung Palace Excursion* written during King Yeongjo period called these stone beasts '*cheollok*.' *Cheollok* is described in *Houhanshu* as a mythical animal, which has unicorn and scaled body, and it is known for having the ability to repel the evil.

By the way, how can it subdue the evil with such mischievous expression! It is watching the stream for sure, but its tongue is sticking out as if it is teasing the evil. The stone carver must had a great sense of humor, interpreting the owner of the palace

A *cheollok* sticks its tongue out.

wanted cute and playful animals. "Tut, tut!"

The Heungnyemun compound, which was damaged for the construction of the Japanese Government-General building during the Japanese occupation, was restored in 2001. As it was restored, a waterway flowing through the palace was also recovered. Even though the waterway looks restored, it was only reconstructed superficially. We cannot say that it was restored in the real sense as all the sources of the waterway were thoroughly blocked during the Japanese occupation. Only when it rains a lot,

Water gates of Yeongjegyo Bridge

it serves as a stream. Then the water does not flow naturally;
sometimes the standing water easily gets so muddy that we feel
embarrassed.

However, *maehwa* (winter plum) and Korean cherry blossoms on
the flower beds along the Yeongjecheon Stream are radiant in
the early spring, and columbines and hosta longipes blossoming
in time also welcome us with splendor. It would be wonderful to
imagine how beautifully *maehwa* petals used to be floating down
along the clear Yeongjecheon Stream in former days.

Cheolloks on the stone embankment of Yeongjecheon Stream
are guarding the palace from any bad energy
coming through the waterway.

An Autumn day, when Korean cherry leaves turn
into fine crimson foliage, a *cheollok* is watching the waterway
with a magpie on Yeongjegyo Bridge

3

Geunjeongjeon Hall
Dreaming of Peaceful Era

You have reached Geunjeongmun Gate,
the third south gate of Gyeongbokgung Palace.

Geunjeongmun Gate and Enthronement

Geunjeongmun (勤政門) is the third south gate of Gyeongbokgung Palace, and its compound was the venue where the king would grant regular audiences to his officials. On the royal audiences, the king would pass by Sajeongjeon Hall, under the eastern eaves of Geunjeongjeon (勤政殿) Hall, through the court of the Geunjeongjeon compound, and reach the gate. The king would be seated on the king's throne set in the middle section of the gate, facing south. His officials would line up in the Heungnyemun Gate compound and pay homage to the king. In other words, Geunjeongmun served not just as the entrance, but as the venue where the king's governing began.

The Heungnyemun compound before Geunjeongmun was considered very important since it was where the enthronement was performed. The enthronement ceremony which was regarded as one of the most significant national rites, ushering in a new era, was conducted mostly during the mourning period of the late king. I would say it is not the grand ceremony teeming with joyous festive mood as you would expect. On the sixth day since the king passed away, the heir was supposed to get dressed in his mourning clothes. For the enthronement ceremony, which took place on the same sixth day since the king passed away, the heir changed from his mourning clothes into his formal robes in the mourning hut setting in front of the royal coffin hall, and he was granted the royal seal, a symbol of king's authority. Then he was escorted to Geunjeongmun riding the sedan chair, ascended to the throne by being seated on the king's chair setting up on the gate facing south, and received congratulatory cheers from his officials.

As such, most of the kings went through the simple enthronement at the gate of the main throne hall during the late king's mourning period. For example, some kings such as Jeongjong, Sejong, Sejo, and Yejong ascended to the throne at Geunjeongjeon Hall, not Geunjeongmun Gate, since the former kings abdicated the throne while they were still alive. King Danjong, Seongjong, Seonjo were enthroned at Geunjeongmun Gate because the former kings were already deceased. The new king took the eastern staircase to ascend to Geunjeongjoen, which was named 'accession to the throne.' Afterwards, the new king promulgated the inaugural message to the general public.

The Joseon Dynasty Highly Valued
Civil Administration

To the east and the west of Geunjeongmun Gate leading to Geunjeongjeon Hall, you will find small gates called 'Ilhwamun (日華門)' to the east and 'Wolhwamun (月華門)' to the west. 'Ilhwa' means the splendorous sun, and 'Wolhwa' means the moon. They were literally named after *yin* and *yang* dualism. Records said civil officials used 'Ilhwamun' and military officials used

Ilhwamun to the east and Wolhwamun to the west seen from Yeongjegyo Bridge

'Wolhwamun.'

The Joseon Dynasty fully adopted Confucianism as the basic philosophy for national administration and highly valued civil administration. You will find several features of Confucian ideology reflected on the layout of Gyeongbokgung buildings.

The main axis of the palace divides the whole area from the east to the west based on *yin* and yang dualism. *Yang* refers to east, sun, heaven, spring, male, odd numbers, activeness, brightness, and warmth. *Yin* refers to west, moon, earth, fall, even numbers, passiveness, darkness, and cold. *Yang* is placed over *yin*. Therefore, you will recognize the Confucian ideology even from the arrangement of the rank stones in the courtyard. Joseon Confucianists pursued the civil-dominated administration. For instance, the rank markers for civil officials are in the east (belonging to *yang*) and those for military officials in the west (belonging to *yin*). Civil officials used the eastern section of Gwanghwamun, while military officials used the western section.

The main north-south axis of Gyeongbokgung continues to extend *yin* and *yang* dualism into a basic architectural concept. This vertical axis divides the palace into the eastern and western areas. The eastern area has Geonchunmun Gate, Ilhwamun, Yungmunnu Tower, Manchunjeon Hall, Yeonsaengjeon Hall, and crown prince's residence. The western area has Yeongchumun

Geunjeongjeon Hall seen from Geunjeongmun Gate

Gate, Wolhwamun, Yungmuru Tower, Cheonchujeon Hall, and Gyeongseongjeon Hall. Gwanghwamun, the south gate, is considered *yang*, while Sinmumun, the north gate, is referred to as *yin*. Hyangwonji Pond is square, and its inner islet is round. It illustrates a Taoist view that the heaven is round and the earth is square, and it also shows the concept that people seek the harmony between yin and *yang*.

Now, would you stand in the courtyard over Geunjeongmun? You will see Geunjeongjeon Hall standing on the two-tiered platforms with commanding dignity. Jeong Do-jeon, who made a great contribution to founding the Joseon Dynasty, named the main throne hall Geunjeongjeon (Hall of Diligent Governance), which carries the meaning that the king's diligence should be the top priority of governance. Citing a historical event, he reminded the king of how to rule the nation. He emphasized the king and his officials alike should stage politics only for the people with diligent attitude, denying arrogance and idleness.

Geunjeongjeon was the main throne hall in Gyeongbokgung, and its court was the site for the state official ceremonies, such as king's enthronement, New Year's audiences, crown prince's investiture, auspicious ceremonies for prince, receptions for foreign envoys, and regular audiences. As for the state rituals, Joseon kings held 'Manggwollye(望闕禮),' which was a ritual performed looking toward the Chinese imperial palace from a distance, and accepting ceremony of imperial letters delivered by

Chinese envoys, and received courtesy calls from all the court officials. In the case of ceremonies for receiving state guests called *Billye* (賓禮), the king personally traveled to the Guest Hall of Peace (太平館) to receive imperial delegation, while diplomats from neighboring countries like Japan and Ryukyu (current Okinawa) were received at the main throne hall.

In addition, Geunjeongjeon Hall accommodated the coming-of-age ceremony for crown prince, wedding rituals for queen and for crown princess, and investiture of high ranking officials. Also, the hall was the place where the royal banquets were held to celebrate the Royal Ancestral Rites of Jeogmyo (宗墓) Shrine, or other auspicious occasions of the state.

In its courtyard, the dynasty announced the royal messages, conducted the state examinations, released the list of the successful candidates, and threw parties paying respect to seniors officials.

King's lane of Geunjeonjeon connected with Sajeongjeon

95

"Success in every business comes from diligence,
and idleness leads only to collapse.
Still more, state business is such a serious affair."

Thin granite stones on the Geunjeongjeon courtyard
reveal stately solemnity.

The Courtyard of Geunjeongjeon Hall

The yard of Geunjeongjeon Hall is called the royal court. The courtyard is covered with thin granite stones, *bakseok* (薄石), with the three-lane road installed in the center, and ✿ rank stones placed on both sides of the road. These small stones mark the assigned places of court officials according to their rank at state ceremonies. Civil officials stood on the east side and military

Watercourse runs, drenching the stone surfaces.

officials on the west side, facing each other.

When the royal celebrations were held in Geunjeongjeon, the king moved from his residence (Gangnyeongjeon Hall) to the council hall (Sajeongjeon Hall), passed through Sajeongmun Gate riding a sedan chair, and ascended to the throne in Geunjeongjeon. At that time, it seems that he entered the rear door of Geunjeongjeon and took a seat on the throne. The king granted

❖ **Rank Stones**: Grades of Joseon officials consisted of nine ranks (from the first to the ninth degree). Each rank was divided into jeong (正) and jong (從) like senior and junior, and posts above the junior sixth degree were subdivided into upper and lower, making its total degrees into 30 classes. Ministers of the upper senior third degree or higher were collectively called '*Dangsanggwan* (palace-ascendable ministers),' while officials from the lower junior third degree to the junior sixth degree were called '*Danghagwan* (palace-downward officials)' or '*Chamsang*,' and officials below the senior seventh degree were called '*Chamha.*' Rank stones are markers of ranks from the first to the ninth. Markers between the first degree and the third degree have jeong and jong, and markers below the fourth degree have only jeong. So all 12 markers are standing on each side respectively. '*Dangsanggwan*' literally means the ministers who were authorized to ascend to the hall to participate in discussions of public affairs.

regular audiences to all the government officials on the court four times a month (5th, 11th, 21st, and 25th day).

Only on the royal court of the Geunjeongjeon compound, you can appreciate how solemn and awesome the thin stones out of the roughly hewn granite are. Rainy days may offer you special highlights to enjoy the watercourse flowing southward and drenching the granite stone surfaces near the south-eastern corridor.

Then, what is the use of the iron rings stuck in the thin granite stones around the rank markers? Old European buildings had rings on their outer walls to tie the bridle. Did they possibly have the same use with the European ones? When tourists are asked the question, most of them answer the rings might have

A marquee ring stuck in the thin stones of the court

A marquee ring on the Geunjeongjeon pillar

Painting of the royal celebration held in Geunjeongjeon in 1887 (The National Museum of Korea collection)

European rings to tie horse reins

been used to fasten the horse reins. According to old pictures and *Uigwe* (儀軌, *Royal Protocols*), however, these rings were used to fix the marquee down to keep the sunlight off at the royal ceremonies. You will find them not only on the court, but on the pillars and the green horizontal beams of the hall.

Corridor Buildings of
the Geunjeongjeon Compound

The royal court of Geunjeongjeon is surrounded with corridor buildings on all four sides. All corridor buildings except the northen one have dual corridor structure with pillars in the center. During King Gojong's reign, compartments made by panelling the space between the center pillars were used as offices and storages. Many compartments were made by

Yungmunnu Tower on the eastern corridor

The eastern corridor

attaching wooden panels to the center pillars and setting up doors. You will find traces of the doors on the center pillars. The eastern corridor has Yungmunnu Tower (Tower of prospering literary arts) and the western one Yungmuru Tower (Tower of prospering martial arts). By installing the two towers on both sides, the dynasty materialized the balance of literary and martial arts and emphasized its importance in dealing with state business. Yungmunnu kept some public documents.

Interestingly, the staff from *Saheonbu* (Office of the Inspector- General) would go up to Yungmunnu and Yungmuru, and oversee the officials attending the regular audiences. That is because the two towers are located in the middle of the array of court officials. *Saheonbu* was in charge of inspecting central and local administration, regulating officials' conduct and discipline and impeaching all the officials. In addition, Yungmunnu is the point where the king's carriages

The eastern corridor

were positioned.

When you go to Sajeongjeon from the eastern corridor of Geunjeongjeon, or you see the eastern corridor and the western one from the platform of Geunjeonjeon, you will find another interesting fact on the corridor roofs. The level of the roof as a whole gets lower twice in accordance with the ground conditions. You can find the reason in the ground difference between the northern corridor and the southern one of the Geunjeongjeon compound. First, when the stone base of the corridor buildings gets one step down, it makes around 50 centimeter difference. The stone base has two-step down, and it leads to approximately one meter difference between the northen end and the southern one of the courtyard. Actually, you will not recognize the difference due to the slow slope of the Geunjeongjeon court, which ensures smooth draining. By cutting off the line of the roofs as well as the stone bases, the corridor roofs show changes in the flow and the height of the ground. This technique of handling rooflines was also applied to installing walls on the steep slopes in the same way. It is architectural exquisiteness that adds variations to lines that are likely to be dull and monotonous.

Geunjeongjeon Hall seen from the eastern corridor

The center staircase leading to the stone platforms of Geunjeongjeon Hall, the royal steps, has *dapdo* (stepping stone). *Dapdo* literally means 'stone path the king takes steps on.' Actually, the king passed over the *dapdo* on the royal steps, riding a sedan chair. The *dapdo* in front of Geunjeonjeon has a pair of *bonghwang* (males were called '*bong*' and females '*hwang*') flying around the clouds engraved on it. *Bonghwang* (Chinese phoenixes)

Upper and lower stone platforms of Geunjeongjeon *dapdo*

The *dapdo* on the royal steps and *haechis*

are mystic creatures, nesting in the paulownia tree, eating bamboo fruits, and never hurting any living things. They are such auspicious birds that they show up only in the age of peace and prosperity. You can imagine that the *bonghwang* engraved on the royal step show that the people prayed for a sage king to usher in the peaceful and prosperous era. When you see the carved birds still remaining in the same palace where they were a long time ago, you may think that the Joseon kings truly cared for his people. Otherwise, the birds still in expectation of the advent of peaceful reign may be lingering on a little longer. Unfortunately, the image of the birds is getting more and more blurred and currently in critical condition of disappearing in no time.

On both sides of the *bonghwang* you can see the statues of *haechi*, and on the royal step you will find arabesque patterns engraved. The arabesque designs wished for an everlasting prosperity of the dynasty. It is said that on state ceremonies the

The *dapdo* has a pair of *bonghwang*.

upper stone platform held only '*dangsanggwan* (palace-ascendable ministers),' and the lower platform seated musicians.

Now, at this point would you turn around to face south toward Geunjeongmun Gate before moving to other places? You will feel that the royal court covered with thin granite stones is so stirring when overlooking the courtyard, and that the building layout in a straight line all the way down to Gwanghwamun Gate is so magnificent. You are now facing the south from the perspective of Joseon kings. The platform called '*woldae* (moon watching stand)' in Korean literally means the raised stand on which you can watch the moon. However, the '*woldae*' involved architecturally symbolic significance that it raised the status of the building as the piled-up stylobate.

Would you turn around to face the south toward
Geunjeongmun Gate? The building layout in a straight line
all the way down to Gwanghwamun Gate is so magnificent.

Animal Statues on Newel Posts of the Stone Platform

The stone platforms of Geunjeongjeon have extraordinary decorations, compared to those of other buildings. Shall we take a close look at their designs? Geunjeongjeon has a double platform structure: the upper and the lower platforms. Large stone plinths surround the stone platforms, and lotus-shaped balusters support the octagonal railing stones. The lotus-shaped

Lotus-shaped balusters

Animal statue on newel posts

baluster is such a beautiful supporting stone with beaded jewels tied in the middle and two lotus petals carved in up-down symmetry.

A number of animal statues are situated on newel posts of the upper and the lower platforms of Geunjeongjeon:

First, four guardian animals representing each direction are carved in pairs on the newel posts of the four staircases belonging to the upper stone platform.

Second, Chinese zodiac animals are also placed on the newel posts along the upper and the lower stone platforms. Among the twelve animal signs of Chinese zodiac, however, the rats and the

The monkey statue

horses are standing on their positions, some of them are out of place, and the dogs and the pigs are missing. Out of the carved animal signs, the rats representing the midnight are on the north, and the horses standing for the noon are on the south. Take a close look at the horses. They are so lovely since they look like adorable babies are blinking their eyes. The highlight of the zodiac animals, though, is the image of the monkey. Ahem, she is standing aloof as if she went through all the ups and downs of the world. You almost sympathize with her look, but you can not help but burst into laughter.

Third, the *haechi* families are placed on both corners of the

113

The baby *haechi* is sucking on his mother's breast.

southern stone platform. Interestingly, they are doing their job faithfully as the king's guards in their positions. The babies look so cute being stuck to their mother. Are they sucking their mother's breast? Through the statues you can glimpse into their loyal determination that they will guard the king from generation to generation. '*Hangyeongjiryak*' introduced the animal family as dogs made of stone.

Even though the stone statues on the Geunjeongjeon platforms clench their teeth, loosely pretending to be scary with such looks, you cannot find any grim scary appearance in these animals. Do you remember that on Yeongjegyo Bridge you already came across the humorous *cheollok* that caught you off guard in the serious environment? How hilarious it is to run into such a facial expression in a solemn place like the palace! There is no other way but to figure out that artisans with a good sense of humor created the work with the same expressions as their own. Artisans are supposed to do their work in accordance with their personal taste. The outcome is obvious that such artisans carved their artwork out of such stones.

Red Phoenix on the newel post of the stone platform

When you see some animal statues of Chinese or Japanese Palaces, you will be surprised with their bloody reality and actually get even terrified. As a matter of fact, they should look scary so as to take a dignified shape and intimidate all the approachers to the palace. Granite stone is so hard and rough that you are likely to go against the grain of the stone when you try to make realistic, detailed description out of granite. Stonemasons of Joseon

115

The west of Geunjeongjeon

seem to have been quite aware of the stone features and have allowed the appearance as the rock wanted. The animal statues along Geunjeongjeon demonstrate their expertise that brought out not only crude and rough, but also warm quality from the most common stone found in Korean soil.

The lotus-shaped balusters along the railing of Geunjeongjeon

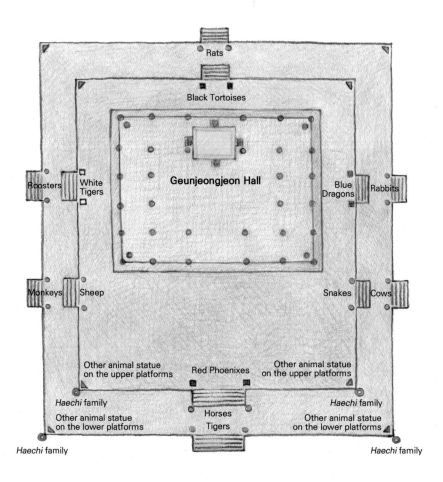

Rats

Black Tortoises

Roosters | White Tigers

Geunjeongjeon Hall

Blue Dragons | Rabbits

Monkeys | Sheep

Snakes | Cows

Other animal statue
on the upper platforms

Red Phoenixes

Other animal statue
on the upper platforms

Haechi family

Haechi family

Other animal statue
on the lower platforms

Horses

Tigers

Other animal statue
on the lower platforms

Haechi family

Haechi family

■ Blue Dragon   □ White Tiger   ■ Red Phoenix   ■ Black Tortoises
● Twelve Chinese zodiac animals (rats, cows, tigers, rabbits, snakes, horses, sheep, monkeys, roosters)
▲ Other animal statue on the upper and the lower stone platforms
○ *Haechi* family

rat   cow   tiger   rabbit   snake

horse   sheep   monkey   rooster   other animal statue

White Tiger   Blue Dragon

Black Tortoise   Red Phoenix   *Haechi* family and other animal statue

You can read Joseon masons' sense of humor from stone animals
on the Geunjeongjeon platforms

Incense Burner

Incense Burners are in the shape of the bulging belly, with three legs and two handles. When official ceremonies were held

Incense burner

here, incense sticks were burned in these large cauldrons fixed on both corners of Geunjeongjeon. According to a picture taken in the early 1900s, these incense burners had lids.

Burning incense is thought of as one of the ways for humans to communicate with the heaven. The three legs signify royal authority, dignity and wealth. Its three legs are patterned after '*sanye* (lion-looking dragon)' who is fond of flames and smoke, and its rim has eight triagrams carved around the edge.

121

Next to the eastern and the western staircases of the lower stone platform, you will find *deumeu,* big water pots made of iron. Now the jar has the plastic lid placed over it for fear that some mindless visitors will toss trash into the pot, and you may have difficulty figuring out its use. Originally, *deumeu* in the palace buildings was a water container to put out fires when

Haechis of the royal steps and *Deumeu*

buildings were set on flames. Construction material during the Joseon Dynasty was mainly wood, which is quite vulnerable to fires, except for roof tiles and foundation footings. Furthermore, palace structure that buildings were connected with corridors made people even more worried about fires. The Joseon people believed fire monsters came from the heaven. They wished that as a fire monster approached a building, it would get scared by its own monstrous reflection on the *deumeu* water and instantly fly away. The supporting stones have a scorched trace which shows that the water was boiled to prevent the water from freezing. Also, it is said that they prepared red-bean porridge in the *deumeu* and shared the porridge on the winter solstice.

Deumeu

Looking into Geunjeongjeon Hall

A Single-story Structure with the Interior Open to the Second Floor

Geunjeongjeon is a two-story building when seen from the outside, but a single-story structure with the high ceiling. The ceiling is supported by higher internal columns, and the floor is covered with traditional bricks. You can notice this hall is a special space for state ceremonies, not an ordinary living space.

Seven-clawed Dragons

With the center part of the ceiling raised a little to make a kind of canopy, small ancons were put together, and colorful decorations were put on to make a canopy ceiling. It is assumed that the canopy ceiling was originated from an umbrella unfolded for noble men. In the middle of the canopy ceiling, a pair of carved dragons are hanging close to the ceiling with small iron rings, displaying their vigorous spirit. The two wooden dragons are plated with gold and let people know that Geunjeongjeon Hall was a venue presided by the king who could

Seven-clawed dragons

wield unchecked absolute power.

Dragons as a symbol of the king's status are invested with the great virtues in all respects. The dragon is described all the time as stern and forgiving as well, if only you do not go against its reverse scale. Legend has it that the dragon has 81 scales over its body. The number of eighty-one means nine by nine equals 81 $(9 \times 9 = 81)$. Nine is the highest yang number. Out of these 81 scales, the dragon has a reverse scale about 30 centimeters long stuck upside under its chin. Dragons keep dignity and generosity of the monarch in ordinary times. However, if someone accidently touches their reverse scale, it readily means death. That is all about how tough it is to convince the other party into something depending on who the other is. Also, that is referring

The brightly-colored throne in Geunjeongjeon catches your eyes.

to the risk one should take if one fails to do so. Especially, what if the other party is the king? Speaking of the reverse scale of the dragon one might get to touch with actions that went against king's intentions···! Throughout the Joseon Dynasty, scholar officials armed with upright mind and spirit had rather chosen death by touching the reverse scale and revived the vital soul of this country through their sacrifice, than just stayed without action for fear of getting to touch the reverse scale.

Dragons of the Geunjeongjeon ceiling has are seven-clawed. From antiquity, dragons were classified by the number of their claws. Dragons as the symbol of the emperor or the king were five-clawed. So, you may not understand why seven-clawed dragons are placed in the hall of Joseon kings. Somebody might have put them on the ceiling to boost the morale of the Joseon people, which makes me a little delightful.

Canopy

Above the throne of Geunjeongjeon, you will find a structure similar to the one placed over the statue of Buddha. The structure is a canopy, which is installed to emphasize the dignity of the royal authority. The canopy is brilliantly decorated with multi-layered wooden brackets. Also, under the brackets of the canopy you can see small poles, and on the ends of the small

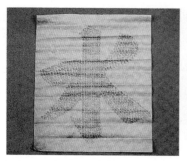

Long paper bearing a big '水' character

Hexagonal silver plates engraved with six '水' characters

poles you will see carved lotus buds. That is the image of lotus buds submerged in water, the meaning of which is to prevent fires.

In the year of 2000, Geunjeongjeon was under extensive repair. When its upper floor was dismantled, some artifacts were found along with the written prayer for the roof-raising ceremony. The ceremony was to finalize the whole procedures of the construction. Among the artifacts, the most interesting item was two sheets of red paper bearing the large '水(water)' character composed of more than 1,000 small '龍(dragon)' characters. In addition, the artifacts included a picture of dragon drawn on the red paper with ink stick and five silver plates on which '水' characters were engraved along each side of the hexagonal plate. Writing '水' character composed of more than 1,000 '龍' characters was intended to ward off evil spirits to stop fire

128

monsters through controlling water with dragons. Dragons served as a symbol not only of royal authority, but also of as a control of water. Wooden structure is quite vulnerable to frequent fires. Ancestors of the Joseon period made all these talismans as an amulet against fires, put them in a groove dug on the beam, and closed it with the lid on the roof-raising ceremony.

Ilwolobongbyeong Screen

The throne of the main hall is elevated high above the floor and has four staircases leading to the throne all around. The armrests and the back of the royal chair are exquisitely carved in brattishing style. Patterns of dragon, lotus and peony are used in carving. Behind the throne you will find the three-folded wooden screen in brattishing technique. The wooden screen is also patterned with dragons, lotuses and peonies.

Ilwolobongbyeong Screen is put behind the three-folded wooden screen. It is also called *Ilwolobongdo* Painting in the form of the picture. Against the backdrop of blue sky, the white moon in the west and the red sun in the east are shining over the five mountain peaks. The screen is unfolding the two pine trees with red trunks, the splash created by cascades of falling water, and the waves raging below the mountains. The sun and the moon grounded on the *yin* and *yang* principle can be

Ilwolobongbyeong Screen

expansively interpreted to mean the whole universe presided over by the king. Five mountain peaks as Mt. Gollyun (a legendary mountain in China) refers to the whole territory the king rules over. They can be applied to Mt. Baekdu in the north, Mt. Jiri in the south, Mt. Geumgang in the east, Mt. Myohyang in the west, and Mt. Bukhan in the center of the Korean Peninsula. The screen is depicting waves as a token of the court where the king would conduct state business, which was derived from the coincidence that the pronunciation of '潮 (meaning of waves)' and that of '朝 (the first character of 朝廷 which means the court) are the same. In short, the *Ilwolobongdo* Painting was based on indigenous faith in mountain gods.

Governing that enables hearty virtue of the king to steep all over the country just like the sunshine is referred to as 'virtuous governance.' The sun and the moon are shining over five mountain peaks day and night. Likewise, the painting wishes 'virtuous governance' will light up every nook and corner around the country day and night, and pray that the dynasty will thrive for eternity. The *Ilwolobongbyeong* Screen as the symbol of the royal authority was set up not just behind the throne of the main hall, but also in the council hall and in the divine chamber where kings' portraits were enshrined. Also, it followed the king anywhere he went, even when he proceeded outside the palace. The *Ilwolobongdo* is the best court painting drawn in folk painting style back in the Joseon Dynasty, using brilliant primary colors.

4

Sajeongjeon Hall
Pondering on the People

"An old saying has it that contemplation leads to wisdom,
and wisdom makes a sage, thus humans can get
such immense use out of contemplation."

King's Council Hall, Sajeongjeon

The name, 'Sajeongjeon (思政殿) Hall,' which means Hall of Thoughtful Governance, was dedicated by Jeong Do-jeon to remind the king of his share of duty as a ruler that he should ponder deeply to distinguish the right from the wrong to look into the condition of the people.

According to the *Annals of the Joseon Dynasty*, on October 7,

Sajeongjeon Hall

135

Cheonchujeon Hall with its fuel holes and chimneys

1395, in the fourth year of King Taejo's reign, Jeong Do-jeon
exhorted that as the king alone holds the highest position, unless
he thoughtfully contemplates to distinguish what is right from
what is wrong as well as who is right from who is wrong, he can
easily fail by seeking only after vain and sumptuous things and
by associating with people who lack decency. Quoting from the
Book of Documents, "contemplation leads to wisdom, and
wisdom makes a sage," Jeong Do-jeon said that humans can get
such immense use out of contemplation, and politely suggested
that the king name his council hall as 'Sajeongjeon Hall,' which
means 'Hall of Thoughtful Governance.'

136

The northern wall of Geunjeongjeon Hall is the corridor building of Sajeongjeon. If you step down from the northern stone platform of Geunjeongjeon, and pass through the Sajeongmun Gate, you can enter the king's office quarters including Sajeongjeon. The compound was king's office quarters where he stayed most of the times to take care of his administrative business.

As Sajeongjeon has a wooden checkered floor without a heating system, it must have been difficult for the king to do his work during the cold winter season. Two auxiliary buildings, Manchunjeon (萬春殿) Hall and Cheonchujeon (千秋殿) Hall, have fire holes to the sides of the stylobates to heat the rooms during the colder months. 'Manchun (萬春)' means 'ten thousand springs,' and 'Cheonchu (千秋)' means 'thousand autumns.' As the 'east' direction corresponds to 'spring' while the 'west' direction corresponds to 'autumn,' the eastern hall is 'Hall of Ten Thousand Springs' and the western hall is 'Hall of Thousand Autumns.' 'Man (萬)' and 'cheon (千)' stand for 'ten thousand' and 'thousand' respectively, meaning 'long lasting and forever,' which expresses wish for the foundation of the kingdom to last for a long time. Cheonchujeon is said to have been used by the scholars of *Jiphyeonjeon*, which was the royal research institute and royal library, during King Sejong's reign.

If you turn around to see the southern corridor building where Sajeongmun Gate stands, you can see a name plate is attached on each door of the long linear corridor buildings which belong to the Sajeongjeon compound. Those were the warehouses for the king to store his private possessions called 'Naetanggo,' and each storage is named in the order of Chinese Thousand Character Classic (千字文) such as 'Cheonjago (千字庫)' and 'Jijago (地字庫),' just as we number things in a numerical or an alphabetical order today.

'Ujago(宇字庫)' belong to the southern corridor building of the Sajeongjeon Hall compound

Painting of Dragons in the Clouds

There is the king's throne laid on the checkered wooden floor of Sajeongjeon Hall. Morning audience like a cabinet meeting called *sangcham* was held everyday. The relevant ministers, senior officials, palace ascendable officials of major offices, royal lecturers, a royal secretary, and chroniclers attended the audience, and discussed state affairs with the king.

King's throne inside the Sajeongjeon Hall

The king also had his learning sessions in this hall with his retainers to enhance his academic level through debates after reading some passages of the Confucian scripture or history. King Sejong never skipped the Royal Lecture called *gyeongyeon* for 20 years, and King Seongjong is also known to have never missed a session for 25 years, strictly observing it three times a day.

It must have been a demanding job for the retainers to catch up with the study of the king's and to serve him who had such an ardent desire for learning.

It is not known exactly when *The Painting of Dragons in the Clouds* hanging on the Sajeongjeon was painted, or if it was originally hung there. The picture symbolically expresses that the king and his retainers are mutually dependent, and should assist one another.

Sajeongjeon Ceiling and *The Painting of Dragons in the Clouds*

The *Annals of the Joseon Dynasty* is the set of records of history covering over 472 years about 25 generations of kings from King Taejo, the founder, to King Cheoljong in a chronological order. Being the longest records of one single dynasty in the world, they were enlisted as 'Memory of the World' by UNESCO in October 1997. With the most abundant and encyclopedic contents, they cover various topics not only on the general state affairs but also on social system and issues, economy, science and arts, religion, astronomy, geography, music, and various facts of natural science including natural disasters, meteorological and astronomical phenomena, and even diplomatic relations among neighboring Northeast Asian countries.

As the system prohibited even the monarch from getting access to the draft history of the ✿ chroniclers, it guaranteed the confidentiality, truthfulness, and credibility of the annals. The *Annals of the Joseon Dynasty*, being printed with movable metal and wooden types and completely preserved while suffering

The *Annals of the Joseon Dynasty* (Korean National Treasure No. 151)

✿ **Chroniclers**: After each morning audience, the king received reports from the royal secretary and the relevant officials on the pending matters. The chroniclers infallibly attended the meeting and recorded every single detail of the reports and their conversation listening to them in person.

Two small low desks laid at either side of Sajeongjeon Hall were for the chroniclers to record every detail of the council presided by the king. It is said that there were a *left chronicler* and a *right chronicler* to record the emperor's remarks and behaviors respectively in ancient China.

Likewise, not only the kings and officials of Joseon could not be free from the chroniclers' recording but also their draft history became one of the most important primary sources to compile the Annals after the death of each king along with *Diary of the Royal Secretariat, Records of Daily Reflection,* and *Chunchugwan sijeonggi* (monthly collection of journals of various government offices maintained by *Chunchugwan,* Office of History Compilation).

Especially, the chroniclers attended all the meetings of the state without fail, and recorded not only all the procedures of discussion and settlement of state affairs without embellishment or deletion but also included subjective commentaries or critiques on particular event or an individual with a straight brush.

Moreover, the regulations regarding history compilation was so stern that nobody else but the chroniclers could read the draft history and Annals, not even the king could. As such, the chroniclers were armed with strict morality, and the confidentiality of their recording work was also guaranteed.

numerous wars not only show the long and advanced level of Korean printing technology and culture, but also is an unprecedented example in the world.

After the compilation of the Annals of the preceding king, four copies were printed, and stored with one set in the archives of the Office of History Compilation in Seoul, the other sets in each of the three Repositories in deep mountain sites built to avoid unforseen damage. During the early years of Joseon, they were in the cities of Chungju, Seongju, and Jeonju. However, after the Japanese Invasions (1592~1598), they were stored in the repositories of the Annals in Seoul, Mt. Mani, Mt. Taebaek, Mt. Myohyang, and Mt. Odae.

Following is from the *Annals of the Joseon Dynasty*, on February 8, 1404, in the fourth year of King Taejong's reign. It shows how much King Taejong was conscious of the chroniclers.

> The king went on a hunting trip with his bow and arrow riding a horse himself. While shooting an arrow at a roe deer, as the horse toppling down, the king fell off the horse, but he was not hurt. Looking around left and right, he ordered, "Do not let the chroniclers know about this [my falling]."

This article shows that no matter how much King Taejong was displeased with the presence of the chroniclers even in the

The roof of Sajeongjeon Hall seen from the stone platform of Geunjeongjeon Hall

king's hunting outing for a personal rest, he could not forbid them from accompanying him as the chroniclers also could not in the least neglect their solemn duty to record all words and deeds of the king's. Probably being too conscious of their presence, King Taejong lost his balance when the horse tumbled down, and fell to the ground. Instead of examining where he was hurt, the first word that he said was, "Do not let the chroniclers know about this [my falling]." Nevertheless, not only did he fail in keeping the chroniclers from knowing the fact, but also it is now even open to public on the internet after 600 years including his very anxious order to keep the chroniclers from knowing it.

Also, through *King Sejong's Annals* on March 2, 1438, in the 20th year of his reign, we can find that once King Sejong consulted with some officials about his reading the Annals of his father, King Taejong, to use them as reference and guide for his governance. However he could not help succumbing to the legitimate logic of the officials and chroniclers at last, concluding not to read them and to guarantee the confidentiality and independence of the chroniclers' job. With their firm conviction and unshakable noble spirit, the officials convinced King Sejong not to read the Annals, as the relevant chroniclers still being alive, they would feel very uncomfortable and insecure, and the future generation would not trust the contents if the king had read them either during or after the compilation of the Annals.

❖ Segeomjeong Pavilion

Over one of the northern minor gates called Changuimun Gate along the Seoul Fortress Wall, stands Segeomjeong Pavilion in a clear valley of a graceful mountain.

According to *Donggukyeojibigo* (comparative review of anthropogeography around Hanyang), it is said that, at the conclusion of the Annals compilation process of the preceding king, they invariably erased the draft documents and revisions in the water of the valley where Segeomjeong stands. They rinsed the papers to get rid of hard evidence of the compilation process as well as to make the paper recyclable.

A classical Chinese poem written by a Joseon civil official named Jo Mun-myeong (1680~1732) depicts the scene of his reciting the poem in the banquet after the draft document rinsing was over to congratulate on the compilation of *King Sukjong's Annals*.

How can we dare to express the achievement of heaven with a trivial brush?
Ah! The great virtues of the preceding King amount to those of 100 kings.
Having completed ten-year-long Annals compilation process,
   now that all the draft documents have been rinsed on this leisured day,
   we are about to have a feast of cooked rice with side dishes.
Prepared having an outing by the stream in this evening,
   the food is all the more delicious,
   while the gurgling sound of the stream
   plays sweeter tunes than Geomungo Lute.
Gazing at the completed books in person,
   it seems that the long and hard labour was only a dream,
   and tears of gratitude and joy run down from my eyes.

King's lane of Sajeongjeon continues all the way to
Gangnyeongjeon and Gyotaejeon Halls.

The sundial in Gyeongbokgung Palace is presently installed in a small yard of Sajeongjeon Hall.

The '*Angbuilgu*' literally means 'an upward looking sundial in the shape of a concave cauldron.' It was first invented by Jang Yeong-sil during the reign of King Sejong telling not only the time as a clock, but also 24 solar terms as a calendar. On the concave surface of *Angbuilgu*, 13 horizontal lines stand for 24 solar terms, and many vertical lines tell the time with the position of the shadow of the pointed gnomon called *yeongchim* which is set to point to the due north. Over the long period of Joseon, several types of *Angbuilgu* had been devised and improved. On the south rim of the cauldron, silver writings are inlaid that Hanyang is located at 37°20' N, which shows the advanced level of science to have already determined the geographic latitude of Hanyang.

King Sejong not only installed *Angbuilgu* in each royal palace and in front of Jongmyo Shrine, but also on the bustling street near Hyejeonggyo Bridge, where Gwanghwamun Post Office is located currently, so that common people could also know the time.

Now, would you like to learn how to read the time?

❖ **How to read *Anbuilgu* sundial**

1. Pour some water through a small hole on the concave surface. The sundial is set even, when the water filled in the cross shaped frame where the four legs stand does not overflow.

2. Hanyang's location 37°20' N is marked on the south rim of the sundial.

3. The shadow needle is pinned down at an angle toward the due north.

4. The horizontal lines stand for solar terms, and the vertical lines stand for the time of the day ranging from 5 a.m. to 5 p.m.

5. 24 solar terms are divided into two groups and marked at either side of the rim of the sundial. On the east rim of the sundial, solar terms from summer solstice to winter solstice, and on the west rim, from winter solstice to summer solstice are marked next to each applicable horizontal line.

6. The top horizontal line stands for winter solstice while the bottom horizontal line stands for summer solstice, and the other 11 horizontal lines are parallel to these lines.

Time is read as follows.

1. One hour is divided into four quarters.

2. The middle vertical line stands for 12 o'clock noon.

3. The time shown on *Angbuilgu* is the real solar time measured at the real location of Korea which is 127°E. (Presently Korea adopts 135°E according to the Greenwich Mean Time.)

4. The earth orbits around the sun rotating 14.5° tilted from its own axis.

5. To know the Greenwich Mean Time, correction figure calculated under the above conditions should be added to the real solar time.

Adjusting table (in minutes)

Date	Jan.	Feb.	Mar.	Apr.	May	Jun.	Jul.	Aug.	Sep.	Oct.	Nov.	Dec.
1~10	35~39	46~47	45~43	37~33	29~29	29~31	35~37	39~37	32~28	21~19	15	20~26
10-20	39-43	47~46	43-40	33~30	28	31~33	38~39	37~35	28~24	19-17	15-17	26~30
20-30	43~46	46~45	40~37	30~29	28~29	33~35	39	35~32	24~21	17~15	17~20	30~35

The gnomon of this sundial *Angbuilgu* is pointing at about 2 p.m. in the real solar time past the seasonal line of 'beginning of winter.' Adding 17 minutes of correction figure which is applicable to the dates of 10~20 in November, the Greenwich Mean Time is about 17 minutes past 2 p.m. Allowing a small margin of error, it still surprises us with its accuracy.

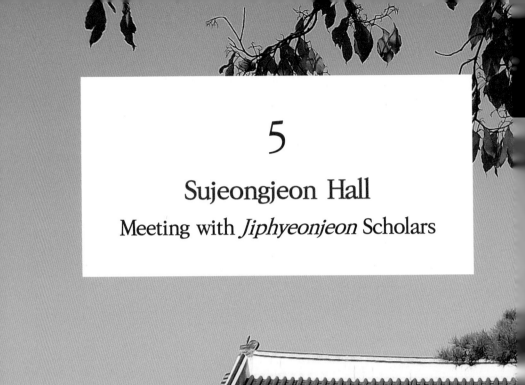

5

Sujeongjeon Hall
Meeting with *Jiphyeonjeon* Scholars

Wooden floored corridors placed inside Sujeongjeon Hall
help feel cooler during the summer.

Passing by Cheonchujeon in the Sajeongjeon Hall compound, and passing through a small exit next to Cheonjago storage, an extensive open space appears in the west of Gyeongbokgung. To the south of the grand two-story pavilion Gyeonghoeru stands a hall called Sujeongjeon (修政殿). Around here also was *Jiphyeonjeon* during the early Joseon period, which operated not only as the

Broad stone platform of Sujeongjeon Hall

155

cradle of academic, scientific, and artistic researches but also as the headquarters of civil administration during the reign of King Sejong. It was where the Korean script 'Hunminjeongeum' ('Proper Sounds to Instruct People') was created in the 25th year of King Sejong's reign (1443), and all sorts of scientific instruments including sundials and waterclocks were invented by Jang Yeong-sil, as well as a musical genre called '*Aak*' was organized and integrated by Bak Yeon for royal rituals and court ceremonies.

To the south of Sujeongjeon, there was a water clock pavilion called '✿Borugak,' where the time of the day was measured. To the west corner of the palace was also set up an astronomical

The stone marker set up on the site of Borugak where Jang Yeong-sil installed a water clock.

✿ Borugak and *Ganuidae*: In the 16th year of King Sejong's reign (1434), a water clock pavilion called 'Borugak,' and an astronomical observatory, '*ganuidae*' was built. In Borugak Pavilion, the time of the day was measured using a water clock named '*Jagyeongnu*,' the self-striking water clock, as a standard clock. To the west of Gyeonghoeru, *ganuidae* was built to observe astronomical phenomena.

observatory called '✿*ganuidae*' to put on the observation equipment, '*Ganui*,' and observe astronomical phenomena. After Sujeongjeon was restored around the compound of Jiphyeonjeon Hall during King Gojong's reign, it was once used as another council hall, and later served as the Office of the National and Military Affairs Administration, and successively as the Cabinet building.

The high and broad stone platform of Sujeongjeon indicates the high status and importance of the building. Both on the east and the west end of Sujeongjeon, two grooved stones are left as traces of corridors that were linking the hall to the west corridor building of Sajeongjeon, and to the east corridor building of

Daejeonjangbang where the eunuchs stayed. During the Japanese occupation period, Sujeongjeon was used as an exhibition hall, and then in 1966, it was used as a folk artwork showroom, which was the predecessor of the present day's National Folk Museum.

The traces of grooved stones that were linking Sujeongjeon Hall with other halls.

The Government Offices Inside the Palace

From Sujeongjeon Hall to the front of Yeongchumun Gate, the western gate of Gyeongbokgung, wide lawns stretch with a lot of trees planted. As the trees in the palace are tendered with great care, to casual tourists, this area may seem to be a very decent garden with gorgeous cornelian cherry flowers and cherry blossoms especially in the springtime. However, the lawns were where the offices inside the palace used to be located.

On the site, many small administrative offices inside the palace were arrayed. While there were Government Offices Outside the Palace standing along the 'Street of Six Ministries' in front of

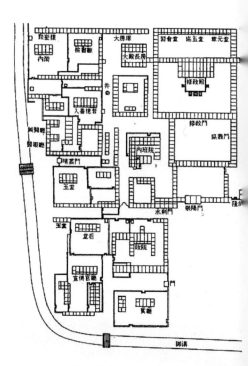

Layout of the Government Offices Inside the Palace on 'Bukgwol-dohyeong', the Map of the Northern Palace, made around 1907.

Spring scenery of Yeongchumun Gate seen from Sujeongjeon Hall

Gwanghwamun Gate, various organizations were also located inside the court to assist the king close at hand. Among them was King's special advisory office *Hongmungwan* or *Okdang*. *Seungjeongwon* was Royal Secretariat, and *Bincheong* was the ministers' meeting and waiting room.

As for military organizations, *Seonjeongwancheong* was the

Office of Royal Guards. *Dochongbu* was the Department of Military and the Palace Garrison. There were also *Daejeonjangbang* where the eunuchs who attended on the king stayed, and the Office of Eunuchs called *Naebanwon* to command them, *Saongwon* which was in charge of making food for the royal family members and supplying the food vessels. '*Gwansanggam*' controlled astronomical observation and equipment such as *ganuidae* as well as the water clock pavilion, 'Borugak.' *Naeuiwon* was the Royal Clinic, and there were many other offices that dealt with royal seals, tent installation, palanquin and horse management.

However, the whole office compound inside the palace was torn down first during the Japanese occupation leaving only one building Sujeongjeon. According to one of the phases of the 40-year-long restoration project, the offices inside the palace will be restored sooner or later between 2013 and 2018.

The office compound inside the palace seen from outside Yeongchumun Gate

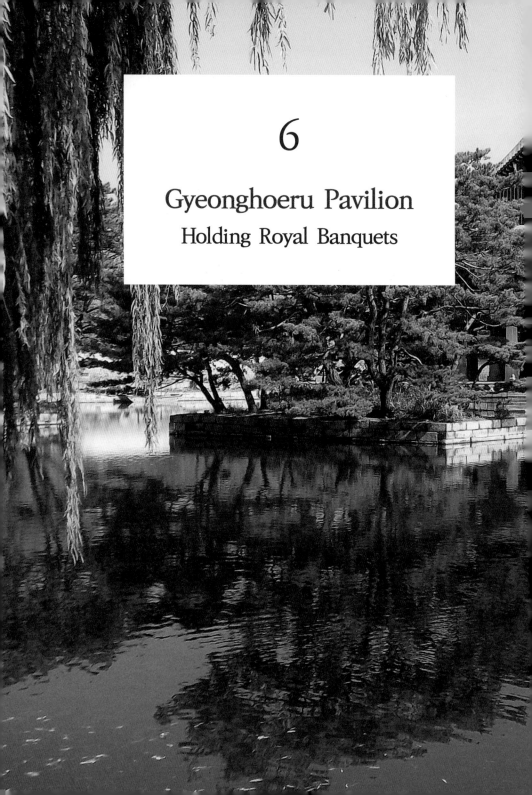

6

Gyeonghoeru Pavilion
Holding Royal Banquets

A shade of summer setting in over the pillars of Gyeonghoeru

To the west of Gangneyongjeon (The King's Living Quarters) and Gyeotaejeon (The Queen's Living Quarters) Halls is located Gyeonghoeru (慶會樓) Pavilion. From the rear of Sujeongjeon Hall, we can get a whole view of Gyeonghoeru and the pond. Gyeonghoeru was a venue for grand state banquets. Previously, there had been a small scale nameless pavilion since the foundation of the dynasty.

Gyeonghoeru Pavilion in the spring

However, when the building began to lean on one side, during the 12th year of King Taejong's reign (1412), the king relocated it westward, making a larger pavilion. At that time, the swampy ground around it was converted into a big man-made rectangular pond, that is 128 meters long and 113 meters wide, and the newly built pavilion was named Gyeonghoeru.

'Gyeonghoe' literally means 'felicitous gatherings' among the king and his subjects. Ha Ryun interpreted, "As I heard before, Confucius said, in reply to the question of Aigong (Duke Ai of Lu, in the Zhou Dynasty of China, 494~467 B.C.), that governance depends on personnel, and that a competent ruler makes it a fundamental rule to employ right personnel, otherwise felicitous gatherings are not possible." King Taejong built Gyeonghoeru originally with a view to entertaining foreign envoys, but the successive kings also used it for a variety of activities, such as holding royal banquets for meritorious officials, and performing rain calling rituals in time of extreme drought.

Along the restored eastern wall of Gyeonghoeru, there are three gates of Igyeonmun, Hamhongmun, and Jasimun. If you think that there is no more to see as you have already seen the front view of Gyeonghoeru Pavilion from the north side of Sujeongjeon Hall, you are mistaken. As a rule, the architecture can be properly appreciated and enjoyed when it is seen from

King's lane installed on the bridge connected to Igyeonmun Gate

the perspective of its master who uses it.

Turning to the eastern wall of Gyeonghoeru toward a narrow alley will actually give you a quite different atmosphere from the one that you felt when you saw the pavilion and the pond from the open side near Sujeongjeon Hall. The high walls surrounding Gyeonghoeru give the pavilion a grave and dignified status.

Among the three bridges to reach Gyeonghoeru, the southern most one connected to Igyeonmun Gate is the king's bridge, because it is only installed with the king's lane. On the newel posts of the three bridges are carved stone animal statues which are known to drive away evil spirits.

Especially on the newel post of the northernmost bridge

The statue of *bulgasari* bearing the bullet marks from the Korean War

connected to Jasimun Gate is carved *bulgasari*. It is a mythological auspicious animal that defends the country from foreign invasions and fires by chewing iron, and by swallowing fire. On the posts of the bridges and on the pillars of the pavilion, we can still see the bullet marks from the Korean War which broke out on June 25, 1950. Wide credence is given to a story that Gyeonghoeru could survive the severity of the war owing to the *bulgasaris* fight with every fiber of their bodies against the force of fire during the war.

Even though we have known that *bulgasari* is a supernatural animal that brings fire under control, we come to thank *bulgasari* again for its loyalty to the country. The bullet marks sporadically left on the pillars supporting the pavilion are roughly concealed with cement.

The wavelets lap against the stone stairs of the islet where Gyeonghoeru stands. There are 48 massive stone pillars supporting the loft. The pillars are designed with a '*minheullim*' style under which the upper sections are slightly narrower, and the outer ones are square while the inner ones are cylindrical. At the time of a large-scaled renovation during King Seongjong's

The pillars of Gyeonghoeru Pavilion designed with a '*minheullim*' style under which the upper sections are slightly narrower.

Artificial islets in the pond of Gyeonghoeru Pavilion

reign (1474), the stone pillars were adorned with dragon sculptures
with flowers, and as the reflections of the dragons looked like
wriggling along the gentle blue waves, and playing hide and seek
up and down the red lotus flowers, foreign envoys from Ryukyu,
which is today's Okinawa, Japan, are said to have exclaimed at
the wondrous sight.

In 1997, in the course of dredging the pond, a bronze dragon
sculpture was excavated. According to *Gyeonghoeru Jeondo*,

170

Ornamented staircase leading to the upper story of Gyeonghoeru

which is a compilation of documents about the pavilion's construction and the floor plan, Regent Heungseon, who was the biological father of King Gojong, dropped two bronze dragons in the north part of the pond when he restored the palace, instead of recreating the sculptures of dragons on the pillars. It was to suppress fire based upon the concept of 'five fundamental elements' of fire, water, wood, metal, and earth. According to the theory, there are 'mutually generating' or 'mutually overcoming' interactions among five elements. As melting metal would generate water, and water would overcome fire, bronze dragons were made and dropped to prevent fires, after all.

To the west part of the pond, two smaller man-made islets planted with some pine trees were created in a measure to let the water circulate around them for prevention of water decay. Record has it that the dethroned King, Prince Yeonsangun made an artificial mound and decorated it with things made of gold, silver, and silk. While hundreds of *'gisaengs,'* professional entertaining women called '✿ *heungcheong'* were performing music, he threaded his way extravagantly in a big golden dragon shaped boat. Going upstairs through the small wooden staircase, you will be attracted to the rolling lines of overlapping roofs of various buildings seen through the ornate window frames. Moving to the west, the rounded but imposing figure of the rocky Mt. Inwang seems to be the spitting image of the famous

✿ The origin of an idiom *'Heungcheong mangcheong'*: *'Heungcheong'* stands for the top class *gisaeng* who performed in the palace during Yeonsangun's reign. *'Mangcheong'* is a counterpart word for *heungcheong* made to rhyme, and the syllable *'mang'* means to perish, die out, or go bankrupt. Yeonsangun (r. 1494~1506) began to select about 100 *gisaengs* of outstanding beauty nationwide, later increasing them to 1,000. As the number of them increased, only a limited number of them could serve near the king. Those who could work near him were called 'Earth-grade' *gisaeng* while the ones who were recognized by the king and spent a night with him were honored as 'Heaven-grade' *gisaeng*. However, due to his unrestrained dissoluteness and extravagance, he was finally dethroned by his half brother, who later became King Jungjong through a coup d'etat, and died in exile. That is how people began to use the idiom *'Heungcheong mangcheong'* to mean the king's perishing after flirting with *heungcheong* or to express an way of wasting excessively to go bankrupt.

The scenery to the west seen from the second floor of Gyeonghoeru reminds the painting of Jeong Seon, *Inwang jesaekdo* (*Clearing after Rain on Mt. Inwang*).

painting, *Inwang jesaekdo* (*Clearing after Rain on Mt. Inwang*) of Jeong Seon (1676~1759), whose pen name was Gyeomjae. To the north, the greenish Mt. Bugak (formerly Baegak), boasts its stately presence, too. When there were no tall buildings like those on Sejongno Street of today, in what shape could the scenery of Mt. Namsan be captured in the gorgeously decorated window frames?

The water inlet inside the eastern wall of Gyeonghoeru
draped with the shade of lush summer greenery

Gyeonghoeru Pavilion analyzed with the *Book of Changes*

It is Korean view of nature and universe to build a house that goes well with nature, following the principles of the universe, and to commune with the nature in the house. All the figures applied to the construction of Gyeonghoeru Pavilion also symbolize the principles and elements of the universe in accordance with *yin* and *yang*, and five elements.

The second floor of the loft of Gyeonghoeru is composed of 35-*kan* square areas.

175

The constructional features of Gyeonghoeru exactly represent the principles of the *Book of Changes*. Gyeonghoeru is a massive two-storied structure composed of 35-*kan* square areas (A '*kan*' is the distance between two supporting pillars, or the square area formed by four pillars). The structure is seven-*kan*-long and five-*kan*-wide, however, if we add the 'Supreme Ultimate (太極)' as one more *kan* square area, Gyeonghoeru is a building of 36-*kan* square areas,

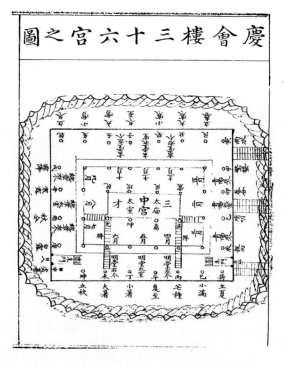

The concept of 36 palaces manifested in *The Floor Plan of Gyeonghoeru Pavilion* according to the *Book of Changes*

accordingly representing the concept of 36 palaces of the universe in the *Book of Changes*. The floor plan is configured of three different levels of sections. The highest center compartment of the loft surrounded with eight inner pillars is of three-*kan* square areas to reflect the 'Three Powers(三才)' of Heaven, Earth, and Human while the eight pillars represent the eight trigrams of the *Book of Changes*. The eight trigrams are ☰ (heaven), ☱ (pond), ☲ (fire), ☳ (thunder), ☴ (wind), ☵ (water), ☶ (mountain), and ☷ (earth). The one step lower section has 12-*kan* square areas for the 12 months of the year while the 64 folding doors hung up between the surrounding 16 pillars symbolize the 64 hexagrams. The lowest outermost wooden floor is made up of 20-*kan* square areas, and 24 pillars supporting the section stand for the 24 seasonal subdivisions.

Moreover, the reason for constructing Gyeonghoeru in the pond located in the west part of Gyeongbokgung Palace was to control fire with water. Water belongs to *yin* as it is cool, dark, and deep. The west direction belongs to *yin* as it is the direction to where the sun sets. Therefore, we can know how thoroughly Confucianism, as the ruling ideology and system of thought of the Joseon Dynasty, is incorporated and expressed in the structure of Gyeonghoeru.

Going upstairs through the small wooden staircase,
you will be attracted to the rolling lines of overlapping roofs
of various buildings seen through the ornate window frames.

Story of Gu Jong-jik

Since Gyeonghoeru Pavilion was a venue exclusively for royal banquets, those who were not invited could not even peek through the high walls from outside. However, there was a lowest ranking official named Gu Jong-jik (1404~1477) who succeeded in sneaking into the pavilion, and even achieved a rapid promotion.

Gu Jong-jik was one of the lowest ranking officials of senior ninth degree in the office in charge of printing and promulgation of Confucian classics. While he had long admired for the beautiful scenery of Gyeonghoeru, he finally sneaked into the pavilion when he was on night duty. Enraptured with the beauty, he did not even know that the king was also visiting the pavilion until he ran across King Sejong. He was first asked for the reason why he sneaked into where he was not permitted to. Gu Jong-jik elucidated the reason, and begged pardon of the king's. Instead of giving him a punishment, King Sejong told him to sing, and being satisfied with his song, the king went on to order him to recite a Chinese history book of Lu, *Spring and Autumn*. Without hesitation, Gu Jong-jik recited it fluently. Being so deeply

The restored eastern wall of Gyeongheoru Pavilion

impressed with his readiness and diligence in his study, King Sejong granted him with an unprecedented promotion to junior fifth degree which meant skipping seven degrees all at once, which would have normally taken for about ten years.

The fact that an unprecedented promotion was granted overnight to a law offender instead of giving a punishment aroused the remonstration of the cabinet members. They might well think the king's special treatment for Gu Jong-jik outrageous and unfair, considering the long period of 450 days that took for an ordinary official to get even one rank promoted proving his personality and ability without making any grave trouble. Being promoted to a junior sixth grade official meant, from that time on, he could attend a morning audience with the king, and was provided with various privileges. Only after passing the higher level civil service examination called '*daegwa*' they could be promoted to junior sixth rank. So promoting him to a junior fifth degree official was much more outrageous. However, it is said that King Sejong turned down the objections of the cabinet members by letting Gu Jong-jik recite *Spring and Autumn* again in front of them. King Sejong's strong will was evidently expressed to show his passion for learning and cherishing hard working officials by setting an example with Gu Jong-jik.

Among all the walls surrounding Gyeonghoeru that were demolished during the Japanese occupation, the eastern and the northern walls are presently restored. If all the walls are restored, will people still feel curious, and try to peek or sneak into the pavilion as Gu Jong-jik once did? People will probably feel too closed and constraint as they have already got used to enjoying the openness of the pavilion for a long time. That is the very dilemma of restoration.

The eastern alley outside Gyeonghoeru Pavilion in the summer

The high walls surrounding Gyeonghoeru give
the pavilion a grave and dignified status.

On the northern edge of the pond of Gyeonghoeru Pavilion, we can see a small pavilion named Hahyangjeong which means the 'fragrance of lotus.' Dipping its two stone plinthes in the water, it retains simple elegance. It was built in 1959 during the President Rhee Syng-man's government. It is said that the chief carpenter Bae Hi-han spent such a long time doing

Hahyangjeong against the backdrop of Mt. Bugak

meticulous work for so small a pavilion that the government employees got angry with him, and pushed him badly to get the work done by the due date. Nowadays, historians may feel displeased with Hahyangjeong because it did not belong to the original Gyeongbokgung Palace. Nevertheless, with its shy posture of sitting, the frail beauty has made it a cultural heritage of its own value even if the short history of 60 years may not come near to the 600-year-old history of Gyeonghoeru.

Gently seated Hahyangjeong by Gyeonghoeru in the summer

The high walls tempt people to peek
into the wondrous Gyeonghoeru.

The pine grove to the west of Gyeonghoeru

7

Gangnyeongjeon Hall
King's Living Quarters

Passing through Hyangomun Gate, the inner court area
begins from Gangnyeongjeon Hall.

At the back of Sajeongjeon Hall, passing through Hyangomun Gate, king's private living space Gangyeongjeon (康寧殿) Hall appears, from which the inner court area begins. The name of the gate 'Hyango (嚮五)' means 'being oriented toward five blessings', According to the *Book of Documents*, '*gangnyeong* (康寧),' which means having physical health and mental peace, is the

Gangnyeongjeon Hall

third and the most representative blessing among five blessings of longevity, wealth, health, love for virtues, and peaceful death at one's home.

The king was said to be able to enjoy all of the five blessings when he straightens up his mind and cultivates virtues. In the name of his living quarters, we can also know what the moral requirements that the people of the day imposed on the king were.

According to the second article on October 10th, 1395, in the fourth year of King Taejo's reign, Jeong Do-jeon suggested that the king name his living quarters as Gangnyeongjeon, citing from a Confucian classic, the *Book of Documents*. He said that the king could enjoy all the five blessings when he achieved the third blessing, *'gangnyeong,'* which means 'having physical health and mental peace,' and that the prerequisite for enjoying five blessings was to achieve 'Supreme World Ordering Principles (皇極).' They were thought to be established when the king straightened up his mind and cultivated virtues. Jeong Do-jeon said that the king should take caution not to be too idle even when he was resting alone in his own dwelling place, giving an example of Duke Wu (武公) of Wei (衛). One of his poems, which was written to make strict precaution not to fall in an idle life, was cited by Jeong Do-jeon for the king to follow the example

Gangnyeongjeon Hall

of him. In the poem, he said he always made a kind and gentle look, and tried to stand on his good behavior even when he was alone in his room. Jeong Do-jeon concluded that the reason why Duke of Wu enjoyed longevity over 90 years old was because of his endeavor to keep his reverence and prudence all the while whether he was with others or was alone.

Gangnyeongjeon was king's private living space where he dwelt and took a rest or slept comfortably. However, he also used the hall to take care of his daily duties, such as summoning his close ministers or holding banquets for royal family members.

The structure of Gangyeongjeon Hall with the big open
wooden floor hall in the middle, and two rooms at either side,
each being arranged in the checkered '井' layout

The Roof without the Dragon's Ridge

Entering the Gangnyeongjeon Hall compound, the roof of Gyeonghoeru Pavilion is seen to the west, and a beautiful and harmonious composition work made up of the lines of the roofs and the protruding corners of the eaves of various buildings outstretches against the backdrop of the sky.

Gangnyeongjeon is not installed with a roof ridge called

The roof lines of various buildings in the west side seen from the Gangnyeongjeon court.

The roof of Gangnyeongjeon without the roof ridge seen from the back side of Sajeongjeon

'*yongmaru*' which literally means 'a dragon's ridge.' When a building is built without a dragon's ridge, two horizontal ridge beams are installed to place rafters on, and the rooftop is covered with curved L-shaped tiles. The distinct reason for not installing a dragon's ridge for sleeping quarters has not been firmly established even though there are various speculations.

First, we may infer that the important sleeping quarters could be distinguished easily from a distance in an emergency. Second, according to a popular version of speculation, people say that the dragon's ridge is not installed to prevent another dragon at

196

the roof ridge from suppressing the real dragon to which the king, who wields absolute power, was compared. However, it is only a speculation in that we see many commoners' houses without a dragon's ridge in China, even though China shares a lot of concepts with Korea. It would be rather reasonable that we construe the reason was to avoid installing such a heavy man-made structure *yongmaru*, which might disconnect the flow of natural energy *qi*(氣) by covering the rooftop with curved L-shaped tiles. At any rate, Korean palace construction features intrinsic characteristics of Korea as well as abides by the principles of the ancient Chinese palace construction.

Stone platform of Gangnyeongjeon Hall

Gangnyeongjeon is built on a high stone platform, *woldae* with broad front stage at the front, and stairs at either side and at the front side of the stone platform. *Woldae* is an extended stone platform of a building which can be used to hold fairly all sorts of events, such as big or small scaled banquets for royal family members and royal relatives, when

The fuel hole of Gangnyeongjeon

the *woldae* is veiled with a tent. In addition, someone might have awaited the official decision about his or her punishment kneeling down on a straw mat on the *woldae*.

After a fire broke out in Changdeokgung Palace in 1917, to rebuild the burnt living quarters of the king's Huijeongdang and the queen's Daejojeon Halls, Japanese dismantled Gangyeongjeon and Gyotaejeon Halls in Gyeongbokgung to use them as the building materials for Changdeokgung Palace. The present Gangnyeongjeon and Gyotaejeon Halls in Gyeongbokgung were rebuilt in 1996 based upon *Gunggwolji* (The descriptive record of royal palaces), *Bukgwol-dohyeong* (Map of the Northern Palace), *Joseon gojeok-dobo* (The illustrated records of Joseon antiquities and relics compiled by Sekino Tadashi of Japan between 1915 and 1935), and the report sources of the excavation sites.

Snow-covered roofs of Sajeongjeon and Geunjeongjeon
seen beyond the southern corridor buildings of Gangnyeongjeon

Roof Figurines

If you look at the protruding corners of the eaves of Yeonsaengjeon and Gyeongseongjeon Halls from the stone platform of Gangnyeongjeon Hall, you can see small figurines set in a row. You must have seen them from when you first entered Gyeongbokgung Palace on the roof of each building or gate. However, this place is where you can see them most clearly from the closest distance, and they are called *japsang* which means

Roof figurines and the guarding net, *bushi* on Gangneyongjeon Hall

Five-pronged spikes

Sharp spikes to keep birds from perching are also found on the buildings in Europe.

sundry figurines.

They are the characters in *Journey to the West*. The first one at the front is the Buddhist monk Xuanzang, and the next ones are Monkey King, Pig Monster, Half Water Demon in order. They are placed on the roofs of the palace buildings to drive away evil spirits, as the strongest group in the novel that defeated all the evil spirits in the world on their journey to India, in search for Buddhist Scriptures and to bring them to Tang. The postures not only of the Buddhist monk, Xuanzang, but also of the Monkey King look very majestic. Chinese roof figurines are composed of a Taoist hermit and auspicious animals like Dragon, Chinese Phoenix, Lion, and Seahorse, but Korean roof figurines are set to ward off evil spirits.

Gyeonghoeru is the biggest building in Gyeongbokgung

201

composed of 35 compartments, which is seven-*kan*-long and five-*kan*-wide. Naturally, the number of the roof figurines is the highest among them as eleven. They are usually set in an odd number, and the bigger the size of a building is, the higher the number tends to be as the line of the protruding corner of the eave gets longer.

You can also find there is a net called *bushi* surrounding brackets under the eaves of the roof to prevent birds from perching on them, and getting the multicolored painting, *dancheong* dirty. On the brackets that were technically difficult to be covered with *bushi*, five-pronged sharp spikes are stuck.

The gable roof of Gangneyongjeon Hall

Yeonsaengjeon and Gyeongseongjeon Halls

Among the five buildings in the Gangneyongjeon Hall compound, the eastern small bedchamber is called Yeonsaengjeon (延生殿) Hall while the western one in the opposite side is called Gyeongseongjeon (慶成殿) Hall. Their names also reflect contrasting concepts of *yin* and *yang.* 'Yeonsaeng (延生)' in the east refers to greeting the revival of all things in the spring

Yeonsaengjeon, the eastern small bedchamber in the Ganagneyongjeon compound

Gyeongseongjeon, the western small bedchamber in the Gangnyeongjeon compound

while 'Gyeongseong (慶成)' in the west stands for jubilating perfection and harvest in the fall. To the left of Yeongsangjeon and Gyeongseongjeon are Yeongildang (延吉堂) and Eungjidang (應祉堂) Halls respectively both meaning 'receiving blessings.'

According to the *Annals of the Joseon Dynasty*, on Octer 7, 1395, in the fourth year of King Taejo's reign, Jeong Do-jeon explained the reason why he suggested those small bedchambers be named as Yeonsaengjeon and Gyeongseongjeon. As for the fundamentals of the heaven and the earth, all living things are born in the spring, and bear fruits in the autumn. Therefore, he

King's well

intended to remind the sage king of his duty, as a ruler of everything on behalf of the heaven, to implement the principles of the nature in his governance. If the king follows the movement of celestial bodies, he would be able to 'revive (生)' people with 'benevolence (仁)' and 'nurture (成)' them with 'righteousness (義).'

Turning to the northwest of Gyeongseongjeon Hall is the king's well. As the king's well is currently topped with a heavy cap stone, it may be hard for us to imagine that the well was used to supply drinking water. However, the cap stone was placed for safety purposes in the course of restoration.

Nevertheless, we can also conjecture that the well had another function for a special ceremony. As a well or a pond in a Buddhist temple was considered as the Underwater Palace of the Dragon King, the king's well in Gangnyeongjeon can also be interpreted as the well of the Dragon to which the king was symbolically compared to.

The cylindrical body of the king's well means the 'Supreme Ultimate (太極),' and the octagonal stone base stands for the eight trigrams of the universe. There are holes in the base to put in the poles of an octagonal gazebo over the well.

A magpie flying over the roof of Yeonsaengjeon on one spring day

Arrangement of the buildings based
upon the Ancient Chinese Astronomy

The ancient Chinese astronomy interprets the position of monarch as the Polaris according to the constellation, and ascending the throne was compared to ascending the Polaris (北極星). As Gyeongbokgung is the primary palace of the Joseon Dynasty, the buildings were arranged following the constellations of 'Purple Forbidden Enclosure (紫微垣).' For example, the main throne hall, Geunjeongjeon corresponds to the Polaris; three buildings in the king's office quarters as Sajeongjeon, Manchunjeon, and Cheonchujeon fall under the 'Three Steps (三台星)' as Upper Step, Middle Step, and Lower Step of the Ursa Major. The five bed chambers of the king's living quarters correspond to 'Seats of Five Emperors (五帝座).' The Purple Forbidden Enclosure occupies the middle of the night sky circled by all the other stars. Ancient Chinese people compared the Purple Forbidden Enclosure to a royal palace on the Earth. 'The Supreme Palace Enclosure (太微垣)' lies to the northeast of the Purple Forbidden Enclosure symbolizing the walls enclosing the garden. In the center of the garden are located Seats of Five

The western alley of the Gangnyeongjeon compound on the way to Igyeonmun Gate of Gyeonghoeru Pavilion

Emperors.

As Three Steps were thought to bring in the peaceful and prosperous time when they get brighter, they had been worshipped and attentively observed by many ancient people, and frequently appeared in many documentary records.

To the northwest side of the Gangnyeongjeon Hall compound, passing through a small side door next to the king's well is found Heumgyeonggak (欽敬閣) Pavilion. 'Heumgyeong (欽敬)' literally means to admire and respect the sky, and furthermore, to tell the people the time. As the Joseon Dynasty was a traditional agricultural society, worshipping the sky, observing the

Heumgyeonggak is located very close to the Gangnyeongjeon compound.

movement of heavenly bodies, and measuring the time precisely were all closely related to the king's authority and power.

Newly built to the west of Cheonchujeon Hall, during King Sejong's reign, Heumgyeonggak housed two important astronomical instruments. The one was '*Ongnu* (Jade Clepsydra, or Heavenly Water Clock).' The other was '*Seongiokhyeong* (A synthetic astronomical water clock mechanism with time and season announcing dolls).' By placing the astronomical clock close at hand, the king could timely observe the movement and phenomena of the celestial bodies so that he could fulfil his duties as a monarch to figure out the time and the season as well as computing the calendar. This means the king ruled the country in compliance with the law and order of the universe. In addition, a concave sundial called *Anbuilgu*, an astronomical observatory called *ganuidae* were also stationed in Heumgyeonggak.

❖ *'Ongnugiryun'* recorded in the *Annals of King Sejong*

According to the *Annals of the Joseon Dynasty*, on January 3, 1438, in the 20th year of King Sejong's reign, Jang Yeong-sil first invented a water clock called *'Jagyeongnu'* with an automatic time announcing mechanism in 1434, and further developed *'Ongnu,'* an automatic astronomical water clock, in January 1438, and dedicated it to King Sejong to be used in the palace. The water clock was housed in Heumgyeonggak Pavilion.

'Ongnugiryun,' also called as *'Seongiokhyeong'* was an equipment that synthesized all the astronomical instruments of that time, combining Chinese astronomical water clock equipped with a water-powered wheel and the Arabic water clock of the middle ages equipped with time announcing dolls. By adding a golden artificial sun, Jang Yeong-sil invented a unique Joseon-style astronomical water clock system. It could update the relative positions of heavenly bodies including the Sun, the Moon, and the other zodiacal constellations.

At that time, Chinese water clocks needed human operation to some extent, however, *Ongnu* of the Joseon era was an innovative water clock that no longer required the reliance on human. In the *Annals of King Sejong*, the reason for naming the pavilion housing *Ongnugiryun* as 'Heumgyeonggak Pavilion' is explained that he could let people know the time and the season by observing the heaven with veneration.

Alley of Yanguimun Gate behind Gangnyeongjeon

Alley of Yanguimun Gate

The chimneys of Gangneyongjeon Hall are built in the northern walls of the compound, which also become the southern corridor buildings of Gyotaejeon Hall. Chimneys are commonly detached to the separate walls of another building in Korean palaces. The auspicious designs of Chinese characters beautifully engraved on the chimneys are 'Cheonsemanse (千世萬

Alley of Yanguimun Gate

歲),' which means thousand and ten-thousands of generations, and 'Mansumugang (萬壽無疆),' which means enjoying long life respectively to the right and to the left of Yanguimun Gate.

The *ondol* structure as a system which heats the building by making a fire in the fuel holes is always equipped with chimneys including smoke vents. However, most of the chimneys in the buildings of Gyeongbokgung are built in the corridor buildings surrounding the main building, by which the smoke can exit farther passing the lengthened underground flues. The chimneys are so neatly treated, contrary to the common recognition as dirty and drab structures with black soot. The sense of beauty decorating the chimneys with auspicious designs are very outstanding. Even to those who do not comprehend the Chinese character patterns, the designs seem to be beautiful modern abstract works.

The chimney engraved with 'Mansumugang'

216

The chimney engraved with 'Cheonsemanse'

8

Gyotaejeon Hall
Queen's Living Quarters

When you see Yanguimun Gate and Gangnyeongjeon Hall
from the stone platform of Gyotaejeon Hall,
you can see the king's lane finally stops
in front of the queen's living quarters.

Passing through Yanguimun Gate
toward Gyotaejeon Hall

The king's lane continues from the back of Gangnyeongjeon Hall to Gyotaejeon Hall through Yanguimun Gate. The name of

The king's lane at the north side of Gangnyeongjeon

the gate means the beginning of the queen's space who will conceive the future king by the principles of *yin* and *yang*. From Yanguimun, the queen's living quarters as well as her office quarters began where she dwelled and administered all the females as the state mother. She granted all the female officials' ranks to '*naemyeongbu*,' which means ladies living inside the court and '*oemyeongbu*,' which means ladies living outside the court including wives of the royal relatives and the officials. Senior first grade was given to the consorts of the king, and the

221

other subsequent ranks were granted to the other ladies like *sanggung* (court lady), and *nain* (court attendant).

The king's lane started from inside the Heungnyemun Gate finally stops in front of the queen's living quarters. By this time, we get to be reminded that our browsing Geongbokgung has reached fairly deep in the palace. Gyotaejeon Hall is indeed located in the deep place being called as the nick name of '*gujung gunggweol*' or 'Ninefold Royal Palace.'

A view of Gyotaejeon Hall through Yanguimun Gate

222

By only taking a glance over the glazing bars of the doors and the decorations along the corridors, we can see the buildings in the queen's living quarters are very elaborately decorated for the queen. 'Gyotae (交泰)' means accomplishing the peaceful and prosperous era by achieving the harmony between the heaven and the earth, and between *yin* and *yang*. The name of Gyotaejeon (交泰殿) originated from the eleventh hexagram '*tae*

(泰, ䷊)' among the 64 hexagrams in the *Book of Changes*. The hexagram '*tae*' is the combination of '*gon* (坤, ☷)' placed at the top representing *yin* or Earth and '*geon* (乾, ☰)' placed at the bottom representing *yang* or Heaven so that *yin* and *yang* interact best. '*Yin*' refers to things related with earth, female, darkness, stillness, and downward moving nature, while '*yang*' refers to things related with heaven, male, brightness, dynamics, and upward moving nature. Therefore, as *gon* and *geon* attracting each other like two poles of magnets, the hexagram '*tae*' is interpreted as a living thing sprouts in the falling rain when the earth and the heaven meet each other and are united

Verandas of Gyotaejeon Hall

Door muntins of Gyotajeon Hall

224

The west part of Gyotaejeon Hall

in one amid thunder and lightening of delight.

When the king visited the queen's living quarters on a designated auspicious day, the king and the queen spent the night together in the east bed chamber. The name of Gyotaejeon contains their wish for the birth of a wise and healthy prince who could make sturdy foundation of the dynasty.

The original Gyotaejeon built during the King Gojong's reign in 1869 was dismantled for its timber to be used to rebuild the burnt queen's living quarters in Changdeokgung after a big fire. The present Gyotaejeon in Gyeongbokgung was restored in 1995.

Children peeking through a small gate
like in *Alice in the Wonderland*.

A small side door under a loft leading to fuel holes in Gyotaejeon

On the way to the rear garden of Gyotaejeon Hall, Amisan
Mound made up of terraced flower beds, passing through
Jaeseongmun gate along the western corridor building, we can
see Hamwonjeon (含元殿) Hall. This hall was deeply related with
Buddhist rituals during the early Joseon Period, and it was also
where Crown Prince Danjong dwelt after his father King Munjong

Hamwonjeon Hall

passed away in 1452.

Hamwonjeon is located deep inside among the living quarters of the palace. Although the Joseon Dynasty chose Confucianism as its ruling ideology, the royal family still revered Buddhism and held Buddhist rituals in Hamwonjeon. According to the *Annals of King Sejo*, there are many records that eye-finishing touch ceremonies for installing a statue of Buddha as well as Buddhist ceremonies were held, and that *sarira* was also enshrined in Hamwonjeon Hall. As King Sejo had to get rid of his own brothers and nephew to gain and guard the kingship, he may have tried to be consoled for his indelible remorse by holding Buddhist services in Hamwonjeon.

A rear garden of Hamwonjeon Hall

Terraced flower beds behind Hamwonjeon Hall

The sculptures on the surface of stone mortar on the back of a turtle outstandingly depict the wriggling of dragons

230

A Well in the Queen's Living Quarters

To the west of Hamwonjeon Hall is a small kitchen, and next to it is a beautiful royal well for the queen. When the *aengdu* (Korean cherry) on the flower beds blossom in the spring, and flutter to the ground like snowflakes, the scene arouses our imagination of seeing court attendants drawing water with a bucket from the well, and hearing their pleasant laughter.

Not only in Gyeongbokgung Palace, but also in all the other Joseon Palaces, *aengdu* trees are particularly planted a lot. According to a collection of essays called *Yongjaechonghwa* by an early Joseon scholar Seong Hyeon, while King Sejong had hard time chewing food with weakened teeth due to diabetes, he could especially eat well sweet and soft *aengdu* fruit. So the crown prince who later became King Munjong planted a lot of *aengdu* trees as shrubbery in the palace. King Sejong praised,

The well arouses our imagination of seeing court attendants drawing water with a bucket and hearing their pleasant laughter.

"Not only my eyes are pleased to see the gorgeous flowers and the fruit as beautiful as jewel, but also my mouth is pleased to taste the sweet fruits." Recalling the crown prince's filial piety toward King Sejong, the pretty *aengdu* feels even more lovely.

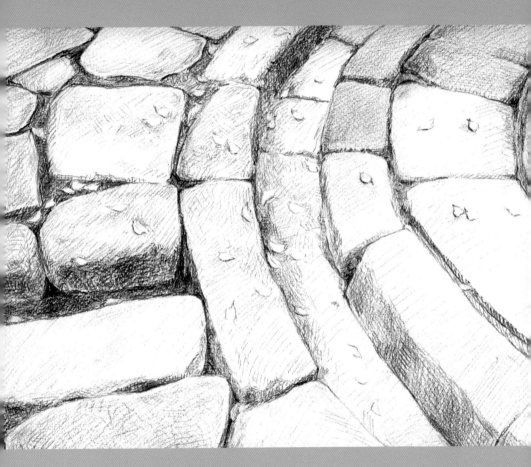

Aengdu flower petals fluttering around the well like snowflakes······

Hang-a of Amisan Mound

Passing through Hamhyeongmun Gate at the back of Hamwonjeon Hall, we reach the peaceful and cozy rear garden of Gyotaejeon Hall which is called Amisan Mound (name originated from Mt. Emeishan of China). When the red royal azaleas bloom in the spring, the view of flower beds in Amisan Mound seen from the open windows of wooden floor in Gyotaejeon is dazzlingly

Hamhyeongmun Gate

beautiful.

Amisan Mound is a small mound of flower beds made up of four tiered stone terraces upon which the soil excavated from the pond of Gyeonghoeru Pavilion is filled, and seasonal flowers and trees were planted for the queen to enjoy change of four seasons.

There are several mountains named Mt. Emeishan in China, and the most famous one is in Shandong Province which is considered as a fairyland where Taoistic hermits live. At the lowest terrace, there are two lotus flower shaped stone mortars of which rim toads are carved on. According to an ancient Chinese legend, Hang-a swallowed the elixir of immortality given to her husband by the Queen Mother of the West, and ran away

A lotus flower-shaped stone mortar with toads carved on the rim

The cozy and peaceful rear garden of Gyotaejeon

to the moon, but turned into a toad. Hence Amisan Mound is the world of the moon where a goddess of the moon lives.

Also about the halfway up the terraces are two more 'large' ponds made of stone of which names are Nakhadam (a pond where the sunset sinks) to the east, and Hamwolji (a pond containing the moon) to the west. Actually they are only two small square stone mortars with the names evoking our poetic sentiment to imagine the brilliant glow of the sunset and the glaring moonlight. The queen also must have imagined of strolling in the Taoist fairy land like the goddess of the moon, Hang-a.

Spring flowers as beautiful as eyebrows of Hang-a,
a goddess of the moon

Halfway up the terraces of Amisan Mound are two 'large' ponds.
One is 'Hamwolji (a pond where the sunset sinks),' and
the other is 'Nakhadam (a pond containing the moon).'

Chimneys in Amisan Mound

As Amisan Mound is a space for females, we can see elaborately decorated flower-patterned brick walls and chimneys. On the upper terraces of the flower beds stand four chimneys. When they are seen first by strangers, they are not easily recognized as chimneys. Red tiles are laid hexagonally a little taller than people, and topped with rooftiles. There are four

Spring in Amisan Mound

smoke vents in the shape of a house in the center of the roof.

The *ondol* system is planned for the smoke to pass through the long underground flues and exit through the smoke vents of the chimneys on the stone terraced flower beds for thermal efficiency and backdraft prevention.

On each side of the chimneys are inlaid patterns to drive away evil spirits. They are dragon face, *bulgasari*, and auspicious

A chimney in Amisan Mound

patterns like ten-longevity symbols, four gracious plants, '卍' meaning ten thousand, and honeysuckle vines turning the somber image of a chimney into a beautiful work of sculpture. On the facets of the chimneys are a scroll of painting of many *maehwa* (winter plum) flowers depicted with a bird heralding the coming of spring, bats bringing in blessings, and cranes also embellishing

240

the mound in the painting. I wonder whether there is any other people in the world that decorate chimneys so beautifully and appreciate them as treasures.

Naming a small artificial mound as Amisan Mound where Taoist hermits live shows the poetic sentiment of Korean ancestors. Furthermore, evoking the reflections of the sunset and the moonlight reveals elevated level of culture that embraces the surrounding scenery into the heart.

Geonsungak Pavilion Interpreted
by Geomancy

Not only was Amisan Mound formed to enjoy the beautiful scenery, but also a more deep meaning can be discovered according to *pungsu* (*fengshui* in Chinese) as Amisan Mound itself is the shape of a *maehwa* flower blooming on the ridge of Mt. Bugak receiving the vital energy, *qi* (氣) flowing all the way from Mt. Baekdu (the highest mountain in the Korean Peninsula worshipped by Koreans

A view of Geonsungak Pavilion

A terraced flower garden of Geonsungak Pavilion

A rear view of Geonsungak Pavilion

as a divine mountain). To the east of Amisan Mound, connected to the back side of Gyotaejeon Hall is Geonsungak Pavilion which was made as a baby delivery room of the queen. Combining characters 'Geon (建)' meaning robustness and 'Sun (順)' meaning gentleness, the name expresses their wish to have a healthy baby in harmony between *yin* and *yang*.

The great vital energy starting from the Baekdudaegan Mountain System flows along the Hanbuk Mountain Range, runs through Mt. Bukhan and Mt. Bugak, and finally reaches Amisan Mound. Geonsungak is built right on the spot where the queen could have a birth of a crown prince receiving the vital energy of Mt. Baekdu to realize the wish of the dynasty.

243

Geonsungak Pavilion built for the queen to have a birth of a crown prince receiving the vital energy of Mt. Baekdu to realize the wish of the dynasty

The flower-patterned brick walls to the north of Geonsungak Pavilion clearly show the elaborate decoration for the beautiful queen dwelling in the pavilion. Also, through the frame of the eastern small arch gate Yeonhwimun, enters the beautiful view of flower-patterned brick walls of Jagyeongjeon Hall.

Railing of the back veranda of Geonsungak Pavilion

Through the frame of a small arch gate, Yeonhwimun,
enters the beautiful view of Amisan Mound.

Flower-patterned brick walls of Jagyeongjeon Hall
seen from inside the Yeonhwimun Gate

Flower-patterned brick walls adorned with various designs
are found around the Gyotaejeon Hall compound.

Wickerwork pattern on the wall as a symbol of
happy occasions in the house

Leaves of apricot trees turning golden on the site of Jamidang Hall······

As the leaves of apricot trees turn golden,
the autumn in the palace gets deeper.

9

Jagyeongjeon Hall
Enchanted with the
Flower-patterned Brick Walls

Shade of Summer seen from the western wall within
the Jagyeongjeon Hall compound

Jagyeongjeon Hall Dedicated
for Queen Sinjeong

To the east of the site of Jamidang Hall is located Jagyeongjeon
(慈慶殿) Hall. Jagyeongjeon Hall is a queen mother's residence
which was dedicated for Queen Sinjeong also known as Queen
Dowager Jo, who was the adoptive mother of King Gojong.
Queen Sinjeong was the crown princess of Crown Prince

A stone animal guarding Jagyeongjeon Hall

Hyomyeong who was the first son
of King Sunjo. Even though her
husband passed away before he
became king, she could become
queen when her son, King
Heonjong granted his father with
the posthumous title of King
Ikjong. Unfortunately, since both
her son Heonjong and the
succeeding king Cheoljong died
without leaving an heir, Queen
Dowager Jo, as the eldest senior
of the royal family, adopted King

Mansemun Gate

Gojong as her son, and made him succeed the throne. He was the second son of Yi Ha-eung, later Regent Heungseon. However, as King Gojong was only twelve, too young to take care of the state affairs, she ruled the country from behind the bamboo screens, and transferred the whole power to Prince Regent Heungseon to administer the country. Jagyeongjeon Hall was once used briefly as the council hall for King Gojong after the queen dowager's regency was over.

The name 'Jagyeong' originated from the 'Jagyeongjeon Hall' which was built in Changgyeonggung Palace by King Jeongjo in

Jagyeongjeon Hall and its summer loft Cheongyeonnu Pavilion

A ceiling of Jagyeongjeon Hall

257

the year he got enthroned for his mother Lady Hong of Hyegyeonggung, posthumously Queen Heongyeong. It means 'wishing the benevolent mother to have happy occasions.' The main gate of Jagyeongjeon Hall is Mansemun Gate praying for long life.

Hyeopgyeongdang Hall

Jagyeongjeon is quite a big residence comprised of a summer loft Cheongyeonnu Pavilion, Hyeopgyeongdang Hall, and Bogandang Hall at the back, all connected with corridors. Even though the front yard is now wide open, it seems to have been separated with *chwibyeong* or wooden panels as partition walls. *Chwibyeong* refers to the weaved bamboo frames entwined with vines to divide the sections.

Even though Jagyeongjeon was built in the fourth year of King Gojong's reign (1867), after having been rebuilt many times due to fires, the present one was rebuilt in the 25th year of King Gojong's reign (1888).

Among the palace walls, there cannot be more beautiful wall
than the western flower-patterned brick wall
of the Jagyeongjeon compound.

The flower-patterned brick walls in April make our mind stirring
as apricot blossoms flutter around them.

Dazzling apricot flowers blossoming in the outer yard
of Jagyeongjeon Hall

The flower-patterned brick walls filled with fresh
spring green after the flowers fell

Elaborately decorated flower-patterned brick walls to
the west of Jagyeongjeon Hall

A Flower-patterned Brick Wall
is a Metaphor

Past the Amisan Mound of Gyotaejeon Hall, passing through Geonsunmun Gate leads us to a spacious empty yard. Grass patches here and there mark building sites where the Jamidang Hall compound was located. Seeing the decorations of outer walls of Gyotaejeon and the western flower-patterned brick walls of Jagyeongjeon standing on the site of the Jamidang Hall

The western flower-patterned brick walls of Jagyeongjeon

compound, we can feel for sure how splendid and refined the architecture of Joseon is. As the walls of Gyotaejeon Hall are recently restored, they do not have such quaint beauty as the original flower-patterned brick walls of Jagyeongjeon.

Nevertheless, the meaning of the patterns on the walls surrounding the Gyotaejeon compound and their splendid contrast of the colors are more than impressive.

As the flower-patterned brick walls in the west side of Jagyeongjeon were made at in the latter half of the 1800s, they are one of the most beautiful walls among the Joseon Royal Palace walls. From the designs of the patterns along the walls and

Patterns of a tortoise shell and the patten of '卍' meaning ten thousand

the chimneys, their wish for the Queen Dowager Jo to enjoy a long and happy life can be assumed enough. From the right to the left on the wall, auspicious Chinese character designs are arranged such as '*man* (萬)' and '*gang* (彌)' meaning health and longevity; '*jang* (長)' and '*chun* (春)' are engraved containing wishes for spring to last for a long time when everything comes alive again. Plants are arranged from the right to the left as bamboo, azalea, chrysanthemum, peony, pomegranates, heavenly peaches, and a *maehwa* tree. From the last picture depicting the little bird drowsing on the twig of a *maehwa* tree under the moon light, we can read the flavor of spring that it brought in our

mind. *Maehwa* flowers were commonly called as 'Early Spring Flowers (早春花)' as they first herald the coming of spring with their graceful fragrance of flowers, overcoming the biting coldness of winter.

Maehwa tree and a bird (Terra-sigillate, 2004 by Yi Hyang-woo)

The picture of a *maehwa* tree and the moon on the flower-patterned brick wall

❖ Designs on the Flower-patterned Brick Walls

Bamboo: It is loved by the Joseon literati due to its integrity that keeps its leaves green during the cold winter. Yun Seon-do praised it as an ever-green plant referring to its hollowed stalk as greedless in his poem "Ouga (Song of five companions)."

Bamboo and a wickerwork pattern

Azalea: With its beautiful shape and colors, it has been popular, and especially a dethroned king Yeonsangun let 10,000 azalea trees planted and tended in the rear garden of Changdeokgung Palace.

Azalea and the pattern of '卍 (ten thousand)'

Chrysanthemum: Chrysanthemums wait without flowering until it begins to frost while other flowers are in full bloom, and they finally bloom in the late autumn, overcoming the first cold spell. Therefore, they stand for endurance and faithfulness. It is also a flower of fidelity and seclusion loved by a famous poet named Tao Yuanming of the Jin Dynasty in China.

The pattern of '卍 (ten thousand)' and chrysanthemum

Pomegranate: Many seeds in the red pocket of the ripe fruit mean fertility, especially having many sons.

A tortoise shell pattern and pomegranate

Peony: It symbolizes wealth and honor, and has been called as the king of flowers.

Peony and an auspicious pattern of Chinese character '禾=年 (years)'

Heavenly Peach: According to *The Classic of Mountains and Seas of Shanhaijing*, the Queen Mother of the West Xi Wangmu living in the Mt. Kunlunshan in the distant west side of ancient China had the elixir of eternal life, and heavenly peaches were also believed to prolong life for thousands of years.

Heavenly peaches and an auspicious pattern of Chinese character '長 (to live long)'

Designs of bats and honeysuckle vines on the side of Ten Longevity Chimney

Bat: Patterns of bats with their wings spread are inlaid onto the walls of the chimneys here and there in Gyeongbokgung Palace. Chinese word for a bat is '蝙蝠.' The second Chinese character '蝠' is pronounced same as that of '福' for 'happiness' or 'blessing.' Therefore in the East Asian Chinese Character cultures, bats are commonly used as a pattern for wishing happiness. As bats are also known to live long, they mean longevity, too. Five bats stand for five blessings of longevity, wealth, health, love of virtues, and peaceful death. They are also seen in the ornaments for ladies and architectural ornaments, too.

Honeysuckle: It stands for strong vitality and prosperity as the vines sprawl endlessly and have a tenacious hold on life enduring long winter. The arabesque design of honeysuckles has been used not only on the flower-patterned brick walls, but also on the sides of stairs, door frames, clothes, and ornaments.

The pattern of broken ice shows splendid harmony
among various flowers, butterflies, and bees on the series of
broken pieces in the composition.

A pattern of broken ice on the flower-patterned brick wall
of Jagyeongjeon Hall

A Crane design on the to right and left of the chimney facade

Dragon face on the top center of the chimney facade

Bulgasari on the bottom of the chimney facade

A Bat design on the sides of the chimney

Ten Longevity Chimney along the northern wall of Jagyeongjeon Hall (Korean Treasure No. 810)

Ten Longevity Chimney

There is Ten Longevity Chimney along the northern wall to the backyard of Jagyeongjeon Hall. There is no such chimney as looks like we commonly expect it to be. The Ten Longevity Chimney is actually a big beautiful wall of a picture.

Even though there are ten underground smoke flues from different buildings in the Jagyeongjeon Hall compound, being

Cranes, tortoises, and elixir plants of eternal life (enlarged picture of the middle part of the chimney facade)

Ten longevity symbol patterns decorating the chimney

surrounded with one-picture wall of ten longevity patterns, they do not look like chimneys. Only when we see the ten smoke vents in the shape of small houses at the top can we guess they are actually chimneys. At either side on the top facade of the wall are two cranes with elixir plant of eternal life in their mouth, and between the cranes is a relief of a dragon face as a symbol of protection from evil spirits. At the left and the right on the bottom facade of the wall are two *bulgasaris* as a symbol of suppressing fires.

Ten longevity symbols are inlaid to wish the queen mother to have a long life without any disease. They include sun, clouds, mountains, rock, water, pine trees, crane, deer, tortoise, and elixir plant of eternal life. On the right side of the wall, the scene depicting ducks sharing love in the lotus pond with grapes next to them metaphorically means fertility as the fruit of their love.

276

Scene of ducks sharing love in the lotus pond
(A ceramic work enlarging the right part of Ten Longevity Chimney,
Terra-Sigillate, 2004 by Yi Hyang-woo)

Will there be anywhere else that we can feel
full autumn better than here?

By the northern wall of the Jagyoengjeon compound,
on one late autumn day when yellow ginkgo leaves were falling off······

The wall tinted with the shade of yellow ginkgo leaves

The eastern wall of the Jagyeongjeon compound

A restored gate showing solid proportion and aesthetic beauty along the eastern wall of the Jagyeongjeon compound, moved from where it belonged as a small southern gate in the upper story of Yeongchumun Gate.

Royal Kitchen in Charge of Meals for the Royal Family

Seen to the south from the Mansemun Gate of the Jagyeongjeon compound, on the quite extensive area, is the restoration site of the royal kitchen that had been in charge of food for the royal family. Close to the living quarters of the king's, the queen's, the queen mother's, and the crown's were located the biggest inner and the outer royal kitchens.

The royal kitchen was in charge of meals for the royal family. On the principle, the kitchen was supposed to be located near the living quarters, however, there were several other kitchens elsewhere. The inner royal kitchen prepared the royal meals of breakfast, lunch, and dinner, and the outer royal kitchen prepared refreshments and rice cake for small and big banquets in the palace. There were court ladies and attendants

The plan of royal kitchen restoration based upon *Bukgwol-dohyeong*

The inside of royal kitchen restoration

who were separately in charge of the meals and the refreshments.

Two different royal kitchens were located side by side which prepared meals and refreshments. There were court ladies who prepared the meals and who served them. Among the three court ladies who served the royal food called *sura*, the oldest court lady was a taster called *gimisanggung* who was in charge of test eating. Another one among the court ladies helped opening or putting on the lid of the tablewares, and the third one prepared and served the stew. On the other hand, male professional cooks called *daeryeongsuksu*, were in charge of royal banquets. Their job and the skills were handed down from generation to generation.

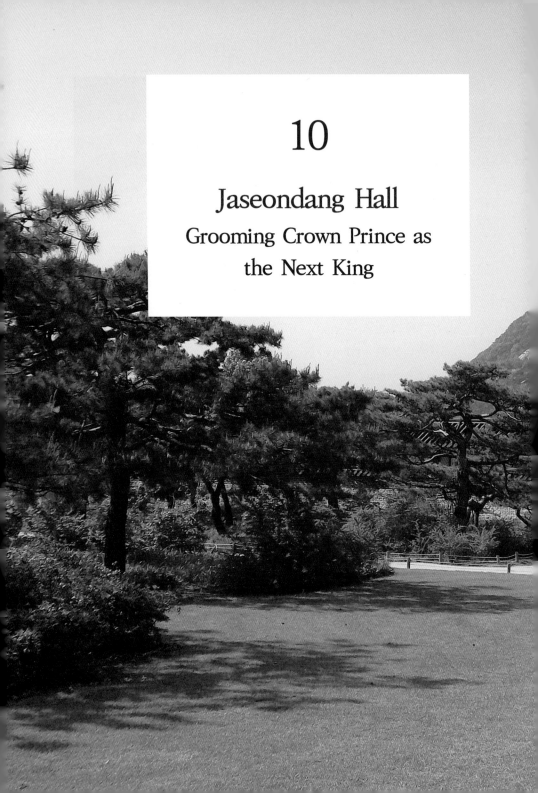

10

Jaseondang Hall
Grooming Crown Prince as the Next King

Geunjeongjeon and Jaseondang Halls viewed from Geonchunmun Gate with the backdrop of distant Mt. Inwang.

The Crown Prince's Quarters, Jaseondang Hall

Jaseondang (資善堂) Hall which is located near the east gate, Geonchunmun, in Gyeongbokgung Palace is the crown prince's residential quarters. It is called 'Donggungjeon (東宮殿)' which means royal residence located in the east side of the palace. The east side symbolizes spring when all things in the universe come back to life: for example, the reason for having the crown

Jaseondang Hall

Jaseondang area, viewed through Igeukmun Gate

prince's investiture in the spring is because it is the season when energy restores.

'Jaseon (資善)' means 'to nurture one's good nature.' In here, King Munjong spent twenty years as the crown prince. Crown Princess Gwon, whose posthumous title was Queen Hyeondeok, gave birth to King Danjong on July 23 in 1441, in the 23rd year of King Sejong's reign, and died the next day. If the queen had not died so early, the tragedy of her brother-in-law, King Sejo, usurping her son's throne might have been prevented. Later, after King Gojong restored Gyeongbokgung, his crown prince (later Emperor Sunjong) also resided in here.

Bihyeongak Hall

Donggungjeon is located in the east side of Geunjeongjeon and Sajeongjeon Halls, and its area was divided into Jaseondang and Bihyeongak (丕顯閣) Halls. Jaseondang was the crown prince's and princesses' residential quarters, and Bihyeongak was the

The crown prince's study room of Bihyeongak

crown prince's office quarters. In front of Donggungjeon, there were two offices which took responsibilities for educating and guarding the safety of the crown prince: one was Chunbang (春坊) which educated him, and the other was Gyebang (桂坊) which guarded him. Thus the crown prince was well prepared to be the next king.

289

Jaseondang Hall is the crown prince's and
Princesses' residential quarters.

A small gate on Jaseondang Hall's outer yard

Where Is the Palace's Outhouse?

It is not easy to find an outhouse in the palace. Sometimes, when we need to use it while we are touring the palace, we come to wonder where outhouses awere located in the palace long ago. Kings and queens were provided with portable toilets, '*maewooteul*,' which means a frame of *maewoo*. *Maewoo* is a rainy season around the middle of June to the beginning of July, when *maehwa* (winter plums) are fully ripened, so they are ready to

Two outhouses located between Jaseondang and Bihyeongak

Four outhouses located in the left of Igeukmun Gate

fall like rain drops. What about others who needed to use the toilet? How did they release their physiological necessity? It is one of the frequently asked questions by the tourists.

Long ago, there must have been many outhouses in several places, but during the Japanese occupation, the palace had been so severely destroyed that it is not easy to find their traces. However, we can refer to the *Map of the Northern Palace* or the *Painting of the Eastern Palaces* and infer the original appearance of the outhouses. According to the *Map of the Northern Palace*, there were twenty eight areas of outhouses in Gyeongbokgung. Donggungjeon area was heavily damaged during the Japanese occupation, but as it was restored in 1999, two outhouses in between Jaseondang and Bihyeongak were also restored. Now, not only these two but also four other outhouses are restored in the east of Bihyeongak. But many tourists never notice that these are outhouses because they are colorfully decorated with multicolored painting called '*dancheong.*' They do not appear to be outhouses at all like the way we imagine.

293

The outer yard of Jaseondang Hall

Leaving Jaseondang Hall and walking toward the northwest of the Jagyeongjeon Hall compound, where Hamhwadang and Jipgyeongdang Halls are, in the left side of the road, there is an uncommon stone pillar engraved with an arabesque design; that is *Punggidae* (風旗臺).

Punggidae (Korean Treasure No. 847)

Punggidae was one of the scientific measuring tools like a sundial and a rain gauge installed in the palace for the purpose of astronomical and meteorological observations. These tools are good examples which show how great effort the Joseon Dynasty, which conceived agricultural production ability as foremost basis of the state, devoted to observing the changes in weather condition. There was a groove on top of *Punggidae* where a flag was fixed, so that the direction and the speed of the winds could be measured.

11

Hamhwadang and
Jipgyeongdang Halls
Immersed in Day Dreaming

There is Yeongjimun Gate, which makes people lower the head
to look into the Hamhwadang area.

Hamhwadang and Jipgyeongdang Halls

There are quite a few mulberry trees on the right side road going toward Hyangwonjeong Pavilion from the north of Jagyeongjeon Hall. When the season of mulberries falling to the ground comes, the road takes color purple. Then the road full of big blue lilyturfs, which bloom under the shade of mulberry trees, is such a beautiful site. From the back of Amisan Mound to the

Hamhwadang Hall

299

Jipgyeongdang Hall

front of Hamhwadang (咸和堂) and Jipgyeongdang (緝敬堂) Halls, and there once was Heungbokjeon Hall located on these spacious areas. Presently, Heungbokjeon territory is being excavated for its restoration. Heungbokjeon used to be the residence of royal concubines. In 1890, Queen Dowager Jo, whose posthumous title was Queen Sinjeong, passed away at Heungbokjeon. Then in 1917, when inner quarters of Changdeokgung Palace caught fire, Heungbokjeon quarter was dismantled for their restoration.

Jipgyeongdang and Hamhwadang on the north of Heungbokjeon were mainly used as the living quarters of royal

300

Hamhwadang and Jipgyeongdang Halls are connected with three-bay corridor.

concubines. Two halls are connected with three-bay corridor. They have several attached buildings with surrounding walls and gates which suggests these halls had different functions from that of Heungbokjeon. They seem to have been built during King Gojong's reign. While Gojong was staying at Geoncheonggung, he held several receptions for foreign envoys in the halls.

When we visit presently restored Hamhwadang and Jipgyeongdang, the area is so calm that we can feel cozy ambience without being disturbed by someone else. In fact, it would be unusual for other tourists to find such a secluded area and have a peep inside. The area was not that significant historically. However, taking a stroll in the palace does not need to be in the area of historically meaningful; it would be good if they are surrounded by cozy walls, then we can rejoice in contemplation. Sometimes we look around and catch the moment of comfort; at such a moment, the owner of the residence may accost us. That moment is when we find the palace so touching. As though things intend to meet our expectation, if we go out of Yeongjimun Gate, in the small garden is a stone mortar with lotus. On an autumn day, after all lotus withered away, crimson foliage of winged spindles fall into the mortar, creating even more impressive scene than the flowers.

Under the Jipgyeongdang's loft, adjacent to a fuel hole,
is the broken ice-patterned wall meaning prevention of fire.

Crimson foliage of winged spindles fall into a small stone mortar creating more impressive scene than flowers.

A stone mortar next to crimson foliage of winged spindles
behind Hamhwadang Hall

There are several mulberry trees on the right side road of Heungbokjeon site and along the circumference of Hyangwonji Pond where Hyangwonjeong Pavilion is located. Not only Gyeongbokgung Palace but also other Joseon palaces have old mulberry trees, which were related to Sericulture Ceremonies performed by the royalty.

As Joseon kings demonstrated how to cultivate lands themselves to understand farmers' soil, their queens demonstrated how to rear silkworms to appreciate that of textile weavers'. Moreover, the queens performed Sericulture Ceremonies in person with court ladies and officials' wives to encourage silk production.

From long ago, silk weaving by rearing silkworms was considered significant in Korea. Thus every village had a shrine worshipping the goddess of sericulture, Xi Ling (西陵) in Ancient China known to have started silkworm rearing, according to Si Maqian (司馬遷)'s *Historical Records*; on the state level was also built the Altar of Sericulture, then kings and officials performed sacrificial rituals regularly, and queens performed the Sericulture Ceremonies to encourage people silkworm rearing. Accordingly, the ceremony was a state level ritual performed to educate people the importance of silk production.

According to the *Royal Court Protocol of the Queen's Sericulture Ceremony*(親蠶儀軌) which recorded the Sericulture Ceremony performed in Gyeongbokgung Palace in the 43rd year of King Yeongjo's reign (1767), the queen conducted a sacrificial rite to the ancestor of sericulture, then plucked mulberry leaves from five branches; and Crown Princess Hyebin, and the grand crown princess plucked leaves from seven branches, next court ladies and wives of high officials plucked from nine branches.

12

Hyangwonjeong Pavilion
Wafting in the Fragrance of Lotus

The Fall of Hyangwonjeong Pavilion

On the way to Hyangwonjeong (香遠亭) Pavilion, to the east side, you can see the National Folk Museum. The museum was built with eclectic structure, so it was not considered harmonizing with Gyeongbokgung Palace. However people accept the building as it is since it has been there for so many years.

After passing Hamhwadang and Jipgyeongdang Halls, if you see Hyangwonji Pond and imposing Mt. Bugak (formerly Baegak),

The Lotus (Terra-Sigillate, 2004 by Yi Hyang-woo)

you have already reached the northern end of the palace. By this time, you will want to find a bench to rest on.

When summer comes, the pond is full of lotus blossom. There is Chwihyanggyo (醉香橋) Bridge connected to a pavilion. Just as the name of 'Chwihyang (醉香)' suggests, it would be great to be intoxicated by the lotus fragrance.

Would you like to sit on a bench around the pond and appreciate the pavilion thoroughly? In the middle of the pond is a round islet, and on the islet is a two-story pavilion named 'Hyangwonjeong,' surrounded by well-trimmed trees. It is a hexagonal structure with pivoted tile roof finished with a pagoda top, which displays utmost beauty of pivoted

Hyangwonji pond in the Summer

roof. It was built all the more beautifully since the pavilion was dedicated to Queen Min by King Gojong.

Originally here was a small pavilion called 'Chwirojeong (翠露亭)' built by King Sejo (1456). Then in the tenth year of King Gojong's reign (1873), when he was building Geoncheonggung Palace, he improved the landscape of back garden by making an artificial islet in the middle and by constructing a hexagonal pavilion called 'Hyangwonjeong.' The name of 'Hyangwon' was taken from "About Loving Lotus (愛蓮說)" by Zhou Dunyi (周敦頤, 1017~1073, in China), which had a verse, 'The fragrance of lotus gets even more refreshing as it diffuses farther.'

312

Intoxicated by Lotus Fragrance

Mt. Bugak located behind the Gyeongbokgung Palace with blue sky as its backdrop changes its landscape by the season and brings out even more the beauty of Hyangwonjeong Pavilion. If you stand in the south of Hyangwonji Pond, you can see a blue dragon symbolizing Mt. Bugak behind the Hyangwonjeong. The dragon has been watching Gyeongbokgung and the whole city of

Hyangwonjeong Pavilion against the backdrop of Mt. Bugak in the Spring

313

Hyangwonjeong and Chwihyanggyo Bridge built on the south side of the pavilion

Hanyang by the four big gates. Near Mt. Bugak's peak, as two boulders protrude, they appear to be like glaring dragon's eyes. Mt. Bugak was Hanyang City's guardian mountain and located in the north, so it was supposed to symbolize a turtle. Then why do we mention a dragon? According to *pungsu* (風水), the mountain which serves as a passage to energy flow is considered a dragon; and depending on its shape, it can be distinguished between auspicious or inauspicious mountain.

The bridge to enter Hyangwonjeong is Chwihyanggyo Bridge. 'Chwihyang' means the lotus fragrance is wafting far by the wind, and the one who is watching the pavilion has already been

An old picture shows the bridge to Hyangwonjeong Pavilion was built on the north side of the pavilion. The left side of the picture is the north (The National Museum of Korea collection).

intoxicated by the fragrance. Is there anything more delightful than this expression?

Originally Chwihyanggyo was not located in the south of Hyangwonjeong. The bridge was burned during Korean War that broke out on June 25, 1950; thus in 1953, the bridge was rebuilt in the south of the pavilion. At that time Geoncheonggung Palace was all demolished that it had no trace of it; hence, for the sake of tourists entering from the south of Gyeongbokgung Palace, to be able to appreciate the landscape, the bridge was rebuilt on the south side. It would be good to examine the height of the

315

The south side of Hyangwonjeong has stairs leading to the pond to appreciate lotus closely.

bridge which is rather low compared to other bridges. The bents under Chwihyanggyo are all submerged overly into water. This is because the bridge started very low from the islet of Hyangwonjeong without any prop. This point where the bridge was rebuilt has stairs leading to the pond to make possible for the original owner of the pavilion to appreciate the lotus more closely.

Then it would be good to examine the side of pavilion facing Geoncheonggung to resolve this inquiry. King Gojong and the queen strolled around the pond while they were living in

316

Geoncheonggung; thus the original bridge was built to enter the pavilion from Geoncheonggung. If we check out from the side of Geoncheonggung, we can see stone-props still remain today. This proves that the bridge was built on the north side of the pavilion. Moreover, we can verify this from an old picture that the north side of the islet was higher than the south side which made possible to build the bridge higher securing the stability of the bridge.

The area around the pavilion was where the royalty took a rest and was absorbed in reading. Originally the edge of the pond was covered with oak tree hedges.

Stone props are still remaining on the north side of Hyangwonjeong Pavilion as the trace of the original bridge.

Also, the islet has traces of stone-bases to pitch tents on. The pavilion has two stories: the first story is a room with under floor heating called '*ondol*,' and the second story has a wooden floor. The ceiling of the second floor is decorated with lotus and phoenix patterns patterns, making it extremely exquisite.

317

Maple branches with accumulated snow are still holding
the autumn foliage near Hyangwonjeong Pavilion.

The Winter Hyangwonjeong Pavilion is lonesome,
yet the exquisite beauty of it gets even richer.

A True Origin of the Han River

By the time we arrive at the northwest corner of Hyangwonji Pond, we get to see a spring called 'Yeolsangjinwon.' The name was engraved on the side of the spring cover; the meaning was that 'this pond, Yeolsang, is a true origin of the Han River or Yeolsu.' The water from Mt. Bugak gathered in this spring and flowed into Hyangwonji Pond; then the pond water coursed to

Yeolsangjinwon

Yeongjecheon Stream, passed through Cheonggyecheon Stream, and ran into the Han River. Thus the spring was seen symbolically as a true origin. If we verge upon the spring, we can see a small cistern in a peculiar shape. The structure of the cistern was designed to slow the swift flow of water, leading the water gathered in a round dish, and to bend the waterway in the shape of Korean script 'ㄱ', intended to make the pond extremely serene. Then underneath the round dish engraved *yin* and *yang* symbol, so that the water followed the shape of *yin* and *yang* and entered the pond. If we look carefully once again into the spring area, on the bottom of the stone, is engraved a shallow duct to quiet the water flow. The Joseon people created quietude by contemplating upon the silent landscape.

The water gathered in a round dish to bend in the shape of Korean script 'ㄱ'

The water from Mt. Bugak gathered in this spring
and flowed into Hyangwonji Pond.

The Beginning of Electricity in Korea

In the north of the pond is a small stone monument indicating that the area was where electricity was generated for the first time in Korea. On March 6, 1887, in the 24th year of King Gojong's reign, people in the palace officially celebrated lighting up 750 electric bulbs at Geoncheonggung Palace in Gyeongbokgung Palace. At that time, the electricity generating room was set up in the northern corridor building of Jangandang Hall in Geoncheonggung, and generated electric power with Hyangwonji Pond's water, thus turned on light bulbs, and illuminated the area at night. Joseon's electricity inflow was two years earlier than those of China and Japan.

At that time people not only from inside the palace but also outside gathered to watch this wonderment

The stone monument records the beginning of electricity in Korea.

Hyangwonji Pond

from the palace wall, so the area was very clamorous. There were even some reports of court ladies suffering from insomnia due to the loud noise coming from the electric generator and the bright lights from the bulbs. Furthermore, the heated water after cooling the generator flowed back into the pond, causing fish to float with their belly up. Then the people worried that this was a bad omen for the dynasty's future. What people said was due to their ignorance in modern scientific knowledge, but the dynasty's future was substantially nearing its end just as they were concerned.

The day when the Joseon people used pond's water to light up
electric bulbs to illuminate their night……

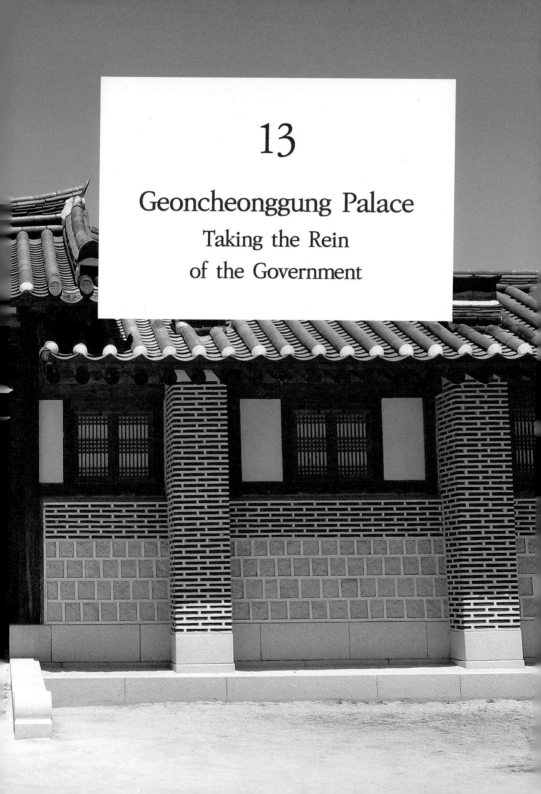

13

Geoncheonggung Palace
Taking the Rein
of the Government

Spring of Geoncheonggung Palace

Geoncheonggung,
a Palace within the Palace

'Geoncheong (乾清)' means 'the sky is clear.' Geoncheonggung (乾清宮) Palace is located to the north of the Hyangwonji Pond area. It consists of several buildings such as Jangandang Hall (The King's Living Quarters), Gonnyeonghap Hall (The Queen's Living Quarters), and Boksudang Hall. As the character 'gung' in the name of 'Geoncheonggung' means 'palace,' it is suggested that it was

The west of Geoncheonggung Palace

another palace within the palace. It was built in 1873 in the tenth year of King Gojong's reign in the northeast edge of Gyeongbokgung Palace. While the grand scale reconstruction of Gyeongbokgung Palace was led by King Gojong's father, Regent Heungson, the construction of Geoncheonggung Palace was led by King Gojong. At that time, the king utilized his private fund to proceed to Geoncheonggung construction project secretly. From the construction of Geoncheonggung, we can conjecture King Gojong's volition to free himself from his father's regency and to lead the government himself. Later the king's subjects found out about the construction of the palace and opposed it,

Long shadows of trees cast on the yard in front of Geoncheonggung

but the king enforced his will. Geoncheonggung was built in resemblance to a noble scholar-official's house with a scale of ninety nine *kan* square areas. And it is similar to Yeongyeongdang Hall in Changdeokgung which has separation between man's and woman's quarters. Geoncheonggung was not finished with colorfully painted decorations, *dancheong*.

After Geoncheonggung Palace was built, King Gojong and Queen Min resided here most of time. However, in 1895 Eulmi Incident occurred when the queen was assassinated. Then in February 1896, King Gojong took refuge in Russian Legation to protect himself from life-threatening danger, which was known as 'Agwan-pacheon.' From that time on, Geoncheonggung Palace lost its original owner; and in 1909 the palace was demolished by Japanese imperialists. Then they built their Government General's art gallery on the site. After Korea achieved the nation's independence, the art gallery was used as National Museum of Modern and Contemporary Art, Korea. It was demolished in 1998 by Gyeongbokgung restoration policy. The restoration of Geoncheonggung began in June 2004 and completed in three years. It was about 100 years after the Eulmi Incident that Geoncheonggung could be finally opened to the public in October 2007.

Muntins on the door of servant's quarters

After Geoncheonggung Palace was built,
King Gojong and Queen Min resided here most of time.

'Jangan (長安)' means 'be in peace for long time.' From the records which mention Jangandang (長安堂) Hall was used for having irregular learning sessions or for meeting with officials, it seems to have functioned like king's office (*pyeonjeon*). Gojong received diplomatic representatives from America, England and Russia and took care of political issues in here. The hall was

Jangandang Hall and its south side Pavilion, Chusubuyongnu

The corridor of Jangandang Hall is connected to the west part of Gonnyeonghap Hall

equipped with the utmost formality and architectural style of high class scholar-official's houses. It is connected to the west corridor of Gonnyeonghap Hall. Other buildings attached to Jangandang are Jeonghwadang Hall as the bedchamber, and Chusubuyongnu (秋水芙蓉樓) Pavilion as a loft. 'Chusubuyong' symbolizes the state of autumn lotus smiling in the water as it is carried on the wind. The style of the pavilion is a loft with protruding corners of Korean eaves which appear to be flying, so the loft look like a beautiful lotus setting on the water as its name suggests. The pavilion resembles Nakseonjae Pavilion in

Changdeokgung Palace, which was King Heonjong's residence. Chusubuyongnu Pavilion was a pair with Sasihyangnu (四時香樓) Pavilion of Gonnyeonghap.

Gwanmungak Hall, which was erected behind Jangandang Hall, in 1873, was first called Gwanmundang. Then in 1875, as its name was changed to Gwanmungak, it was used as King Gojong's library. Originally Gwanmungak was built in a traditional wooden structure, but reflecting the royalty's volition to accept western civilization, it was renovated to a two-story brick building by a Russian architect, ✿A. S. Sabatine (1860~1921); thus it was the first and the only one building constructed in the western style in Gyeongbokgung Palace. However, after Japanese imperialists demolished Gwanmungak in 1901, the site only remains empty at present. Before the demolition of the

✿ **A. S. Sabatine:** Korea's first western architect who built not only Gwanmungak in Gyeongbokgung Palace but also many others, i.e., Independence Gate (Dongnipmun), Russian Legation in Jeongdong, Sohntak Hotel, Jeonggwanheon, Jungmyeongjeon, Dondeokjeon, Guseongheon Halls in Deoksugung Palace. He was the main architect of Western style architectures erected in Modern Korea. At that time, he was residing in Gwanmungak in Gyeongbokgung Palace. In 1895, he witnessed the assassination of Empress Myeongseong and by reporting the Incident to Russian Consulate, he made the assassination known first internationally.

Geoncheonggung area by Japanese imperialists, there used to be an electricity generating station in the northern corridor building behind Gwanmungak Hall. Since 1887 this area was where Korea's electric light bulbs were illuminated, which shows King Gojong's promotion of modernization and its historical significances.

Leaning to the south side wall of the Jangandang compound, a persimmon tree is planted. King Gojong was very fond of persimmons, so the persimmon presented to the king from other localities were called 'Gojong Persimmons.' The present persimmon tree planted there was sent from Sancheong, South Gyeongsang Province in memory of King Gojong.

The electricity generating station in the north of Jangandang Hall and the front of the station is an empty site where Gwanmungak used to be located.

Over the wall of Jangandang,
Hyangwonjeong Pavilion is boasting its beauty.

Autumn scenery of Hyangwonjeong Pavilion beyond the wall
seen from the wooden floor of Jangandang Hall

Gonnyeonghap (坤寧閤) Hall is located in the east side in Geoncheonggung Palace. This was the queen's living quarters. 'Gonnyeong (坤寧)' means 'the earth is peaceful,' which conveys connotation of queen's virtue. To the north of the hall is Boksudang, and attached to the hall is Okhoru(玉壺樓) Pavilion, the south pavilion. Okhoru's east side is separately named

Gonnyeonghap Hall

Okhoru, the south pavilion of Gonnyeonghap

'Sasihyangnu (四時香樓),' which means 'a pavilion where fragrance floats all year round,' already suggesting feminine ambiance.

Hyangwonjeong Pavilion over the wall of Okhoru Pavilion reminds me of Empress Myeongseong. Sometimes I rather feel piercing pain in my heart because its scenery is so beautiful. Around Okhoru is where Empress Myeongseong (Posthumous title of Emperor Gojong's wife, Queen Min) was assassinated in an unutterably brutal way by Japanese at the age of 45. After murdering her, Japanese assassins burned her body to get rid of evidence. In the

The hanging planks engraved with 'Okhoru' and 'Sasihyangnu'

middle of the eastern corridor building of Gonnyeonghap is Cheonghuimun (清輝門) Gate located on the way to a pine grove called Noksan, where her body was burned.

The tragedy that Queen Min was assassinated by Japanese in 1895 is called 'Eulmi Incident.' In 1894, right before the First Sino-Japanese War broke out, King Gojong moved to Changdeokgung Palace temporarily to shun Japanese oppression. Then he came back to Gyeongbokgung Palace within a month and stayed in Geoncheonggung. A year later, Eulmi Incident occurred in Geoncheonggung. The incident was a disgrace for

An alley of Jeongsihap where Empress Myeongseong presumed to have been assassinated

the Joseon people because the mother of the state was assassinated by Japanese in the palace which represented their state authority.

In 1894 Donghak Peasant Revolution occurred in Joseon, which served as a cause for China and Japan to send their militaries to Joseon to quell the revolt. Shortly after that, a war broke out between China and Japan on Joseon soil. King Gojong appointed Kim Hong-jip who was a representative of centrism cabinet, carried out Gabo Reform to regain confidence from the estranged people, and opened the gate to the western civilization

343

Boksudang Hall located to the north of Gonnyeonghap

in full-scale. In 1895, as Japan's victory became certain at the Sino-Japanese War, Japan began to put pressure on the Joseon Dynasty, intervening in the domestic state affairs without withdrawing the military from Joseon. Japan had already disclosed their ambition to gain the whole continent including China and Russia by making Joseon their stepping stone. In an effort to block Japanese forceful intervention on Joseon's politics, Queen Min strived to have good diplomatic relations with Russia. The queen who had keen sense of politics and diplomacy was an excellent partner of King Gojong in every aspect. Therefore her political stance was reflecting King Gojong's intention. However, Japan regarded Queen Min as their stumbling block to their control over the Joseon Dynasty. In the early morning on October 8 under the operation named 'fox Hunt', Miura Goro (三浦梧樓), Japanese diplomatic representative, led members of the legation, itinerant swordsmen, and the military into Geoncheonggung to murder the queen. The murdering of Queen Min by Japanese was witnessed by an American, a Russian, and others. They reported the assassination to other countries' diplomats, thereafter the Eulmi Incident was widely known to other countries.

Now there is no authentic picture or portrait of Queen Min remaining. We can only commemorate her through some dignified portraits painted out of imagination and some records describing her appearance. Queen Min did not meet such a heroic death as she was portrayed in a famous Korean musical, "The Last Empress."

The assassination of Queen Min by Japanese imperialists was shocking both at home and abroad. Domestically all across the country rose the righteous army to revenge Queen's murder. Internationally, condemnation on the Eulmi Incident, which perpetrated by Japanese, got increased. Therefore, in order to avoid international criticism, Japanese government imprisoned the people who committed the assassination for a short period of time. A few months later they released all those criminals including Miura Goro under the pretense of 'lack of evidences.' The assassins including reporters, politicians, and writers shared the same political ambition with Japanese imperialists, and they were playing important roles in Japanese government or society. After Eulmi Incident, they became ministers and diplomatic representatives.

Pilseongmun Gate

Shiba Shiro (柴四郎, 1853~1922), who played the role of bringing in itinerant swordsmen in Joseon to murder the queen with Miura Goro, studied at Harvard University, and graduated from the University of Pennsylvania in economics. He was an active politician and a writer, whose pen name was Tokai Sanshi. There were some other intelligent collaborators who graduated from the Department of Law in Tokyo University, took charge of invading Gyeongbokgung Palace and murdering the qeen, and served as diplomats or major cabinet members. As such, they were the far right politicians in the frontline of Japanese imperialists disguised as civilians. The Eulmi Incident perpetrated by Japanese imperialists was deliberately planned to the minute details.

The posthumous title of ✿ Empress Myeongseong was granted to the deceased Queen Min when King Gojong founded the Great Han Empire and became emperor in 1897.

✿ **Empress Myeongseong**: Isabella Bird Bishop (1831~1904) who was a daughter of a high ranking clergyman in the U.K. visited Joseon four times from 1893 to 1897. During her visits, she met the empress four times, and she described her impression of the empress in her book, Korea and Her Neighbors, as the following: "Her Majesty, who was then past forty, was a very nice-looking slender woman, with glossy raven-black hair and a  very pale skin, the pallor enhanced by the use of pearl powder. The eyes were cold and keen, and the general expression one of brilliant intelligence ⋯ I was impressed with grace and charming manner of the Queen, her thoughtful kindness, her singular intelligence and force and her remarkable conversational power even through the medium of an interpreter. I was not surprised at her singular political influence, or her sway over the King and many others."

Why is the landscape of Noksan viewed from Cheonghuimun Gate
so sad as well as so beautiful?

Retrieved Stylobate Stones of Jaseondang Hall

Cheonghuimun Gate

Jaseondang Hall was the living quarters of the crown prince in Gyeongbokgung Palace, but it became one of many buildings in Gyeongbokgung that were destroyed or dismantled to be sold to Japanese during the Japanese occupation period. A Japanese trading merchant, Okura Kihachiro (大倉喜八郎), purchased the hall and relocated it to his house in downtown Tokyo and used it as an art gallery in the name of 'Joseon Gallery.' But the gallery was burned during the Great Kanto Earthquake in 1923, and only stylobate stones remained. Afterward Kim Jeong-dong, an Architecture Professor of Mokwon University, discovered the stones through his investigation and tracing in the garden of Okura Hotel in Tokyo,

Japan in 1993. Toward the end of 1995, about 110 ton of 288 remaining stylobate stones were repatriated to Korea.

Although the stylobate stones of Jaseondang Hall were returned to Gyeongbokgung Palace after they had been deserted in Japanese land, the stones could not be used for the restoration of Jaseondang because they were burned so badly that they could not serve as foundation stones. Consequently, those burned, smoked and collapsed heap of stones are just left helplessly in Noksan located next to Geoncheonggung Palace. They are still crumbling loosely under the gloomy shade of the forest even now. Of all places on the palace precincts, the stones are seated in the very place where Empress Myeongseong's corpse was burned by Japanese. When we think about the period we lost our sovereignty, our hearts are aching once again. When we lost our country, not only people but also building structures suffered such ordeals.

Repatriated stylobate stones of Jaseondang in Noksan
located on the side of Geoncheonggung Palace.

14

Jibokjae Hall

Reflecting upon Modernization

Autumn leaves tinged with red and yellow seen
over the west of Jibokjae on the road to Sinmumun Gate

King Gojong's Library, Jibokjae

When we go out of Pilsungmun Gate in the west of Jangandang Hall in Geoncheonggung Palace, we can see Jibokjae (集玉齋) and the Gyeongbokgung Palace's north gate, Sinmumun, on the wide area, in the northwest of Gyeongbokgung. Jibokjae was King Gojong's library and was constructed gorgeously in Chinese architectural style. The meaning of 'Jibokjae' is 'a house

Jibokjae

The hanging plank engraved with 'Jibokjae'

where jade is collected.' It had collections of numerous precious books and was used as a library; thus it could be interpreted as 'a house that collects precious books like jade.'

The hanging plank of Jibokjae is hung vertically. It is engraved with collected characters of Mi Yuanzhang (米元章), with his name and seal also inscribed on the left. He was a famous calligrapher in the Northern Song Dynasty. The hall was erected in Chinese style and has a hanging plank where engraved in the collected characters of Mi Yuanzhang. The hall was unprecedentedly built in exotic Chinese style and has *woldae* and *dapdo*. Moreover, the sculptures' facial expression on the *woldae* staircase and *dapdo* is grotesque, and colorfully painted decorations are extremely florid. Dragon heads on the roof are very realistic, different from Korean dragon heads on the ridges of the roof. Jibokjae seems to be one-story when viewed from the outside, but the inside of the building has a loft connected with a passage, making it a two-story structure.

The door frames and multi-colored patterns of Jibokjae are very florid.

Full moon and half-moon windows seen in back of Jibokjae

In back of the building, it has a full moon shaped window, and on both sides of the window, it has two half-moon shaped windows. To the east, the building is connected to Hyeopgildang Hall, which has the shape of Korean script 'ㄱ.' To the west of Jibokjae is connected to Parujeong Pavilion. King Gojong utilized these halls as gallery, library, and reception areas for foreign envoys. In 1893 alone he received diplomatic ministers from England, Japan, and Australia five times in here.

Parujeong Pavilion

A dragon head on top of the roof

A corridor connecting Jibokjae and Hyeopgildang

Animal sculptures on the staircase

The staircase leading to *woldae* in front of Jibokjae

Against the backdrop of Mt. Bugak, Parujeong is on the left,
Jibokjae in the center, and Hyeopgildang on the right.

The Outside of Sinmumun Gate

Behind the Parujeong Pavilion, we can see the palace's north gate, Sinmumun. Traditionally, the gate was kept closed, then only when the king wanted to visit a back garden in the outside of Gyeongbokgung Palace, it was opened. Presently the outside of Sinmumun Gate is the road next to Cheong Wa Dae. Cheong Wa Dae area used to be where the secondary palace or the

Sinmumun Gate seen from the south

The outer view of Sinmumun Gate after restoration. For 1929 Joseon Expo, Japanese imperial government had broken down the wall (The National Museum of Korea collection). From 1937 to 1939, as Japanese imperialists built the official residence of their Governor-General in the area near Sinmumun Gate, the major destruction of the palace was committed.

Goryeo Dynasty was located. But from the beginning of the Joseon Dynasty, King Taejo, the founder of the dynasty, used the area as a back garden of Gyeongbokgung Palace. During King Gojong's reign, the area was called 'northern garden (*bugwon*)' when the total reconstruction of Gyeongbokgung Palace was in progress. There were Yungmundang, Yungmudang, Chunandang Halls, and Ongnyeonjeong and Gyeongnongjae Pavilions, as well as the king's rice paddies for *chingyeongnye* (in-person ceremony of the king's plow to show a good example of a farmer himself). On the higher area was Gyeongmudae where the king could inspect military trainings and could hold banquets. Furthermore, King Yeongjo often used Sinmumun Gate on his way to Yuksanggung shrine, where his natural mother Lady Sukbin Choe's spirit table was enshrined, even though Gyeongbokgung was not restored at all from the Japanese Invasion in 1592.

Japanese imperialists built the official residence of their Governor-General in the back garden outside the Sinmumun Gate when they constructed their Government-General building inside the Gyeongbokgung Palace. Later the residence was used as the first President of Republic of Korea, Rhee Syng-man's official residence and its name was changed to 'Gyeongmudae.' Since the second presidency, the president's official residence and office has been called 'Cheong Wa Dae.'

A view of Mt. Bugak and Cheong Wa Dae
across the road from Sinmumun Gate.

A view of Cheong Wa Dae from Sinmumun Gate

The street between Cheong Wa Dae and Sinmumun Gate

365

Gyemumun and Gwangmumun Gates

On the outside of Sinmumun Gate, if you walk a little to the east along the road in front of Cheong Wa Dae, you can see small gates, Gyemumun and Gwangmumun along the north wall of Gyeongbokgung Palace. Gyemumun Gate was made by stacking up bricks to form an arch. If you walk up a little more, you can see another small gate, Gwangmumun with its name engraved on top of the arch. 'Gyemu' means 'Black Tortoise' in the north; and 'Gwangmu' means 'to expand one's valor.' The character 'mu' meaning 'bravery' was used for the northern gates including Shinmumun Gate. As those small gates seem modest, almost hidden within high palace walls, they were probably used by people who did menial works in the palace. Nevertheless, they rather look much friendlier than Sinmumun or Gwanghwamun Gates which display imposing appearances.

Gwangmumun Gate

If you would like to enjoy Gyeongbokgung Palace in more secluded and romantic ways, I recommend you to walk toward the north by following the east side wall of the palace from the main entrance of the National Folk Museum. If you walk along the palace wall, a road to Cheong Wa Dae appears. The road is quite secluded and poetic. After passing Gwangmumun and Gyemumun Gates, as soon as you see the main gate of Cheong Wa Dae across the road, you would have already approached Sinmumun Gate. Entering the palace through Sinmumun is also possible. The gate is much less crowded than Gwanghwamun Gate. From there you

Gyemumun Gate

can see stately appearance of Sinmumun with its wings spread widely. You can buy an admission ticket and enter the palace from there. Touring the palace in a reverse way, from the north Sinmumun Gate to the south offers a different charm. Of course, it is better to try this route after you have viewed the palace starting from the south, Gwanghwamun Gate first. Anyhow, the reason why I suggest you to view the palace in diverse ways is because the palace will offer you its unique attraction each time.

15

Taewonjeon Hall
Conforming to the Heaven's Way

The shade of pine trees drawn on the wall near Taewonjeon Hall

Sacrificial Ritual Area, Taewonjeon Hall

Taewonjeon (泰元殿) Hall is an area for holding sacrificial rituals, which is located in the northwest of Gyeonghoeru Pavilion. Being located in a secluded area, it is very quiet and unfrequented by tourists. When we step out of Mansimun Gate of Gyeonghoeru Pavilion alley, Taewonjeon with the view of Mt. Bugak on top of it appears. The pine tree forest on the way to

Taewonjeon Hall area viewed through Iljungmun Gate

371

Cheollang, the corridor leading to Taewonjeon viewed through Gyeonganmun Gate.

Taewonjeon makes the atmosphere of the road even more solemn. Looming Mt. Bugak seems to guard the heavens of the Joseon Dynasty with its vigorous energy.

'Taewon(泰元)' means 'the heavens.' This was where the corpse of the deceased royal family members were laid during the state funerals, so it seemed to have been called 'the heavens.' When a royal family member passed away, the state mourning was carried out in Taewonjeon till the funeral ceremony was held at the royal tomb. After the funeral, the spirit tablet of the deceased was placed in Munsojeon Hall for three years before it

372

Cheollang, the corridor of Taewonjeon seen from the west

was finally enshrined in the state shrine, Jongmyo. There were Yeongsajae, Gongmukjae, Hoeanjeon, and Mungyeongjeon Halls which were used as necessary facilities for such sacrificial rituals, and *Sedapbang* was a laundry facility.

The names of the halls and gates all seemed to be referring to revering the heavens and being discreet in behaviors. When we enter Taewonjeon Hall through Gyeonganmun Gate, there is a corridor with a roof called '*cheollang*' across the courtyard connected to the middle of the hall. *Cheollang* evokes much more piety and solemnity than *haenglang*, the corridors built to the sides of the palace.

The reason why King Gojong built Taewonjeon area was to legitimize his kingship, for he inherited the throne being adopted by King Ikjong. He transferred the portrait of King Taejo, Yi Seong-gye, the founder of the Joseon Dynasty from Yeonghuijeon Hall and installed it in Taewonjeon. Afterwards, Taewonjeon was utilized as the royal coffin hall for the deceased Queen Dowager Jo, who enthroned King Gojong, and King Gojong's queen, Empress Myeongseong.

Gongmukjae

After the queen was assassinated in 1895, King Gojong took a refuge in Russian Legation for a year from

Yeongsajae

February 1896. Then in September 1896, he moved the queen's royal coffin hall from Taewonjeon in Gyeongbokgung to a newly built Gyeonghyojeon Hall in Deoksugung Palace. The next year, in October 1897, when King Gojong became the emperor proclaiming the foundation of Great Han Empire, he granted his deceased queen with a posthumous title of Empress

Inner rooms in Taewonjeon Hall

Inner corridor in Taewonjeon Hall

Myeongseong. It was two years after the assassination that her funeral could finally be held in November 1897, at her burial site, Hongleung, Cheonglyangli. Afterwards, King Gojong received his officials in Gongmukjae, one of the anterooms in Taewonjeon.

Taewonjeon Hall now appears solemn which is suitable for its function once served as a royal coffin hall. However, before the restoration, this area was demolished by Japanese imperialists; then not only the area was occupied by Japanese and American militaries but also occupied by Korean Thirtieth Unit of Security Guard of the Capital Defense Command until 1997. Only in 2005, after the rude clamor of the walking military boots disappeared, Taewonjeon was restored to its original solitude as it was in the Joseon Dynasty.

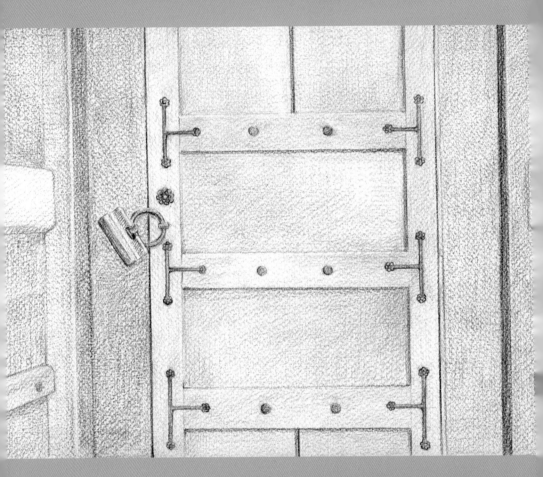

A Small door of Yeongsajae

Leaving Taewonjeon Hall and walking toward Gyeonghoeru Pavilion, there are terraced walls of *Janggo*. If you turn along the walls to the east, you can see the main entrance, Yeseongmun (禮成門) Gate.

Janggo refers to the place where they kept jars of soy sauce, bean paste, and other condiments used in sacrificial rituals and

Yeseongmun Gate

Jars of sauces and condiments in *Janggo*

court banquets. According to the *Map of the Northern Palace* (*Bukgwol-dohyeong*), there used to be two *Janggos*, to the east and the west of Hamhwadang and Jipgyeongdang Halls. This *Janggo* is the one in the west, between Gyeonghoeru Pavilion and Taewonjeon Hall. The platforms of the jars in *Janggo* were built in tiers so that the sauce and the paste might ferment well being exposed to the maximum sunlight. Even in the *Painting of the Eastern Palaces* (*Donggwoldo*), *Janggo* located at the back of Seonjeongjeon Hall in Changdeokgung Palace or Yeomgo, where salt jars were kept, in the west of Tongmyeongjeon Hall in

Changgyeonggung Palace are drawn on the terrace.

The Joseon people put soy sauce in a big jar, salted seafood in a middle-sized jar, and bean paste in a small jar. As Korean ancestors conceived that some disaster would strike if their soy sauce and bean paste changed their flavors, the flavors of the sauces were considered significant. Accordingly, in the palaces, they picked the most auspicious day to make soy sauce and bean paste and performed rituals to wish for good flavors of the sauces and even practiced shamanistic rituals, i.e. stretching a straw rope with hanging red peppers to prevent any malign influence coming into the area. The customs of hanging a red pepper string on a gate for repelling evil, or cutting out the shapes of traditional Korean sock, *beoseon*, from Korean traditional window paper and pasting them upside down on the jars are still practiced by some people even nowadays. The custom started from a humorous notion that worms would not dare approach the jars in fear of being trampled down to death. Not only in the palace but also in commoners' houses, people picked the most auspicious day to make the sauces, and they paid their utmost sincerity. This devotion is still carried on today. People of the past and present conceived that in order to make delicious sauces, the makers must do their best with their whole hearts. Nowadays, we can buy these traditional sauces in a market. But long ago, every house used the sauces to make flavors of food. Therefore people considered the family tradition was stemming from the flavors of the sauces.

The sauce jars (*Jangdok*) are baked in high temperature with special care that they are breathable. So the potters say that the living jars make the flavors of the sauces. *Janggo* in Gyeongbokgung Palace displays 195 jars collected from the whole country. Depending on the climate of the region, the shape of sauce jars can vary from full to slim in stomach area. The jars in the hotter region tend to have full stomach shape: for example, Jeollado Province jars display full shape in the upper part and slim in the bottom, and Gyeongsangdo Province jars tend to be full all around. Jeju Island jars even display orange tone which is the sign of containing volcano ashes. The west *Janggo* in Gyeongbokgung Palace was excavated in 2001, completed its restoration in 2005, and ever since has been opened to the public.

Jars of sauces and condiments in *Janggo* of Gyeongbokgung Palace

Ten Scenic Spots in Gyeongbokgung Palace

What would you remember after your trip to Gyeongbokgung Palace today? So many of you, so many ways. However, here are ten scenic sports to help you cherish the beauty of Gyeongbokgung Palace.

The First Scene

A view of Geunjeongmun, Heungnyemun, and Gwanghwamun Gates in a straight line seen from the stone platform of Geunjeongjeon Hall

The Second Scene

Thin granite slabs, *bakseok*, in the court of Geunjeongjeon Hall

The Third Scene

An auspicious animal on the stone platform of Geunjeongjeon Hall

The Fourth Scene

The rolling line of the roofs seen through the window of Gyeonghoeru Pavilion

The Fifth Scene

A view of roof lines seen from the stone platform of Gangnyeongjeon Hall

The Sixth Scene

The Queen's well at the back of Hamwonjeon Hall

The Seventh Scene

One of the chimneys in Amisan Mound, the rear garden of Gyotaejeon Hall

The Eighth Scene

Flower-patterned Brick Walls seen from the site of Jamidang Hall

The Ninth Scene

Ten Longevity Chimney in the back yard of Jagyeongjeon Hall

The Tenth Scene

The changing view of four seasons around Hyangwonjeong Pavilion

A Chronological Table of Gyeongbokgung Palace History

Year	Regnal year of King	Events
1392	King Taejo 1	In July, Taejo ascended to the throne in Suchanggung Palace in Gyegyeong (current Gaeseong). It was the beginning of the Joseon Dynasty.
1394	Taejo 3	In September, Namgyeong, Goryeo's old temporary palace site was decided as the new palace and ad hoc committee, *Shingunggwol Joseong Dogam* was set up to be in charge of constructing a new palace. On October 28, transferred the capital to Hanyang. In December, under the supervision of Sim Deok–su, the palace construction began.
1395	Taejo 4	On September 29, Jongmyo (in a scale of 64 square *kan* areas including 7–*kan* spirit tablet halls, and other annexes) and the new palace (in a scale of 755 square *kan* areas including 173 square *kan* areas of inner court including living quarters, 192 square *kan* areas of outer court, and 390 square *kan* areas of office quarters) were completed. Gyeongbokgung Palace was completed three years after the dynasty began. On October 7, few days after the palace was completed, Jeong Do–jeon was appointed to name the new palace and its major halls. Gyeongbokgung Palace with Gangnyeongjeon, Yeonsaengjeon, Gyeongseongjeon, Sajeongjeon, Geunjeongjeon Halls, and Geunjeongmun and Omun (Gwanghwamun) Gates were named at this time. During these periods, in the fifth year of King Taejong's reign (1405), Changdeokgung Palace was built as the secondary palace establishing the Dual Palace System, which designated Gyeongbokgung Palace as the primary palace and Changdeokgung as the secondary palace.

1411	King Taejong 11	Built Geumcheon Stream in Gyeongbokgung Palace.
1412	Taejong 12	Built a big pavilion and named it 'Gyeonghoeru'
1420	King Sejong 2	Set up *Jiphyeonjeon*.
1426	Sejong 8	Under the king's order, *Jiphyeonjeon* made names for Gwanghwamun, Hongnyemun (currently Heungnyemun), Iilhwamun, Wolhwamun Gates and Yeongjegyo Bridge.
1429	Sejong 11	Starting from the remodeling of Sajeongjeon and Gyeonghoeru, many buildings were renovated, and some were newly built. While King Sejong resided in Gyeongbokgung Palace during his reign from the eighth to thirty-first year, the palace gained its dignity as the primary palace. Later in 1553, the eighth year of King Myeongjong's reign, the palace went through a big fire, but Gyeongbokgung progressed and was maintained fairly well until Imjin Japanese Invasion broke out.
1592	King Seonjo 25	In April, due to Japanese Invasion in 1592, Gyeongbokgung was burned by Japanese.
1865	King Gojong 2	Under Queen Dowager Jo's order, Gyeongbokgung was decided to be reconstructed.
1868	Gojong 5	On July 2, King Gojong moved in to Gyeongbokgung Palace from Changdeokgung.
1873	Gojong 10	Built Geoncheonggung Palace to the north of Hyangwonjeong Pavilion.
1895	Gojong 32	In Gonnyeonghap of Geoncheonggung Palace, the queen was assassinated by Japanese which is called 'Eulmi Incident.'
1896	Gojong 33	In February, King Gojong and the crown prince took a refuge in Russian Legation (*Agwan-pacheon*).
1897	Gwangmu 1 (The Great Han Empire)	In October, Gojong moved to Deoksugung Palace, thus Gyeongbokgung Palace lost its status as the primary palace.

1910		After Japanese imperialists forcefully annexed Joseon, the palace was devastated systematically, almost losing its original shape.
1912		For the construction of Japanese Government-General building in full-scale, Heungnyemun Gate with its corridor buildings and Yeongjegyo Bridge were torn down.
1915		Under the pretext of commemorating the fifth year of Japanese occupation, Japanese imperialists held Joseon Products Exhibition in Gyeongbokgung Palace, demolishing most of the buildings except for several buildings. Japanese used the exhibition as distorted propaganda that they developed the backward industry of Joseon. At that time the crown prince's residence, Jaseondang Hall was sold to a Japanese trading merchant, Okura Kihachiro.
1916		From June, construction of Japanese Government-General building around Heungnyemun Gate area began.
1917		Most of the buildings in the living quarters of Gyeongbokgung were dismantled and were used to rebuild the living quarters of Changdeokgung, which were burned by a big fire.
1926		The construction of Japanese Government-General building was completed. Gwanghwamun Gate was dismantled.
1927		Japanese imperialists wanted to get rid of Gwanghwamun Gate which was removed in September, but facing the opposite public opinion, it was relocated to the north of Geonchunmun Gate.
1929		In May, dismantled Yungmudang and Yungmundang Halls in the north of Sinmumun Gate and used the building materials to build Japanese Buddhist Temple Yonggwangsa located near the Han River.
1932		In October, Seonwonjeon Hall, where enshrined all the kings' royal portraits of the Joseon Dynasty, was sold to Bakmunsa Temple which was built by

		Japanese to pray for the repose of their assassinated Governor General, Ito Hirobumi (He was assassinated by a respected Korean independence activist and pan-Asianist, An Jung-geun).
1935		Demolished Geoncheonggung Palace, turned the site into the fairground for their exposition to celebrate the 25th anniversary of Japanese occupation of Joseon; such as this, under Japanese imperialists' systematic destruction of Gyeongbokgung Palace, numerous buildings were torn down or sold in auction to Japanese civilians to be used in building their private residences. On the sites where the buildings were removed were filled pagodas and stupas as that were collected from Buddhist temples all over the country.
1995		In August, Japanese Government-General building was demolished. In December, the Gangnyeongjeon and Gyotaejeon compounds were restored. Jaseondang and Bihyeongak were restored in the crown prince's residence.
2001		In October, restored Heungnyemun Gate area including Heungnyemun, Yuhwamun Gates and Yeongjegyo Bridge.
2003		Replaced the high corner columns and totally repaired the roof of Geunjeongjeon Hall.
2004		In October, transferred the National Museum of Korea which used the whole building of former Japanese Governernment-General to Yongsan, Seoul.
2005		Restored the eastern wall of Gyeonghoeru Pavilion and Taewonjeon Hall area.
2006		Restored Geoncheonggung Palace area.
2008		Repaired Hamhwadang and Jipgyeongdang Halls and restored their corridor buildings.
2010		Restored Gwanghwamun Gate area and made Gwanghwamun Plaza.

The Genealogy of the Joseon Dynasty

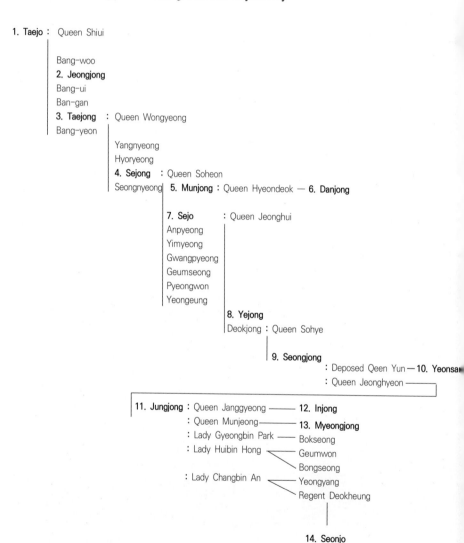

Seonjo : Queen Uiin
 : Queen Inmok ——————— Great Prince Yeongchang
 : Lady Gongbin Kim ⟨ Imhae
                     15. Gwanghae
 : Lady Inbin Kim ⟨ Uian
                    Sinseong
                    Jeongwon —— **16. Injo** : Queen Innryeol
                    Uichang
                                │ Crown Prince Sohyeon
                                17. Hyojong : Queen Inseon
                                Inpyeong │
                                Yongseong │ **18. Hyeonjong** : Queen Myeongseong
                                                    │ **19. Sukjong** : Queen Ingyeong
                                                                      : Queen Inhyeon
                                                                      : Queen Inwon
                                                    : Lady Huibin Jang — **20. Gyeongjong**
                                                    : Lady Sukbin Choi — **21. Yeongjo**

Yeongjo : Queen Jeongseong
 : Queen Jeongsun
 : Lady Jeongbin Yi —— Crown Prince Hyojang
 : Lady Yeongbin Yi —— Crown Prince Sado : Crown Princess Hyebin Hong —— **22. Jeongjo** : Queen Hyoui
                                             : Lady Uibin Seong —————— Crown Prince Munhyo
                                             : Lady Subin Park —— **23. Sunjo** : Queen Sunwon
                                          └─ Crown Prince Hyomyeong : Queen Sinjeong
                                                                    │ **24. Heonjong**
 : Lady Sukbin Im ⟨ Euneon — Regent Jeongye — **25. Cheoljong**
                    Eunsin — Namyeon — Regent Heungseon : Prince Consort Min
 : Lady Gyeongbin Park — Eunjeon
                                                        │ **26. Gojong**

26. Gojong : Empress Myeongseong — **27. Sunjong** : Empress Sunmyeonghyo
                                                        : Empress Sunjeonghyo
             : Lady Gwiin Eom — King Yeongchin
             : Lady Gwiin Yi — King Wanchin
             : Lady Gwiin Jang — King Uichin
             : Lady Gwiin Jeong — Wu
             : Lady Gwiin Yang — Princess Deokhye

389

References

Internets

Korean Britanica, http://www.britannica.co.kr/
Kyujanggak Institute for Korean Studies in Seoul National University,
   http://e-kyujanggak.snu.ac.kr
Institute for the Translation of Korean Classic, http://www.minchu.or.kr
The Annals of the Joseon Dynasty, http://sillok.history.go.kr
The Daily Records of Royal Secretariat of Joseon Dynasty, http://sjw.history.go.kr
Wikipedia, http://ko.wikipedia.org/

Korean Books

Changdeokgung 600 Years (in Korean). Changdeokgung Office, Cultural Heritage
   Administration of Korea, 2005.
Choe, Jong-deok. *Joseon ui Chamgunggwol Changdeokgung.* Nulwa, 2006.
Cultural Heritage Administration. *Gunggwol ui Hyeonpan gua Juryeon 1:*
   Gyeongbokgung. Suryusanbang, 2007.
_____. *World Heritage in Korea* (in Korean). Nulwa, 2007.
_____. *Sunan ui Munhwaje.* Nulwa, 2009.
_____. *The royal palaces and royal shrine of Joseon* (in Korean), Nulwa, 2010.
Gilsang (Best wishes: Auspicious symbols in Chinese art) (in Korean). The National
   Museum of Korea, 2012.
Gunggwolji. Seoul Teukbyeolsi History Publishing Committee, 2nd Edition, 2000.
Gunggwolji 1: Gyeongbokgung, Changdeokgung. Seoul Study Center, 1994.
Gunggwolji 2: Changgyeonggung, Gyeonghuigung, Doseongji. Seoul Study Center,
   1994.
Her, Gyun. *Jeontong Misul ui Sojae wa Sangjing* (in Korean). Kyobomungo, 2001.
Hong, Soon-min. *Wuri Gunggwol Yiyagi.* Cheongnyeonsa, 1999.
Jang, Heon-deok. *Mokjo Geonchuk ui Guseong.* Korean Cultural Heritage
   Foundation, 2006.
Jeong, Jae-hun, et al. *Soswaewon.* Daewonsa, 2002.
Jeong, Yeon-sik. *Ilsang euro Bon Joseon Sidae Yiyagi.* Cheongnyeonsa, 2001.
Kang, Gyeong-seon, et al. *Yiyagiga Yitneun Gyeongbokgung Nadeuri.* Yeoksanet,

2000.

Kim, Dong-hyeon. *Seoul ui Gunggwol Geonchuk.* Sigongsa, 2002.

Kim, Jae-won. *Gyeongbokgung Yahwa.* Tamgudang, 2000.

Kim, Mun-shik and Byeong-ju Shin. *Joseon Wangsil Girok Munhwa ui Got,* Uigwue. Dolbegae, 2005.

Kim, Wang-jik. *Algi Shiwun Hanguk Geonchuk Yongeo Sajeon.* Dongnyeok, 2007.

Kim, Yeong-mo. *Algi Shiwun Jeontong Jogyeong Siseol Sajeon.* Dongnyeok, 2012.

Kim, Yeong-sang. *Seoul 600 Years* (in Korean). Hangukilbosa, 1990.

National Research Institute of Cultural Heritage. *Haksuljosabogo vol 19: Gyeongbokgung Taewonjeonji.* Korea Cultural Heritage Foundation, 1998.

Park, Hong-gap. *Haneul wieneun Sagawani Itsoida.* Garamgihwoek, 1999.

Park, Sang-jin. *Gunggwol ui Wurinamu.* Nulwa, 2001.

Park, Yeong-gyu. *Hangwon euro Ingneun Joseon Wangjo Sillok.* Deulnyeok, 1996.

Seoul Teukbyeolsi. *History Publishing Committee.* Cultural Properties of Seoul (in Korean), 2011.

_____. *Seoul 600 Year History* (in Korean). Munhwasajeokpyeon, 1987.

Shin, Eung-su. *Gunggwol ui Hyeonpan gua Juryeon 1: Gyeongbokgung Geunjeongjeon Jungsugi, Gyeongbokgung Geunjeongjeon.* Hyeonamsa, 2005.

Shin, Myeong-ho. *Joseon ui Wang.* Garamgihwoek, 1998.

Shin, Myeong-ho. *Joseon Royal Court Culture: Ceremonial and Daily Life.* Translated by Timothy V. Atkinson. Dolbegae Publishers, 2002

The National Museum of Korea Collection Yuri Geonpan, Gunggwol. The National Museum of Korea, 2007.

Yi, Sun-wu. *Geudeul un Jeongmal Joseon eul Sarang Hatseulga.* Haneuljae, 2005.

Yu, Bon-ye and Gwon Tae-ik, trans. *Hangyeongjiryak.* Tamgudang, 1975.

Yun, Jang-seop. *The History of Korean Architecture* (in Korean). Dongmyeongsa, 1981.

Korean Thesis

Jang, Yeong-gi. "Joseon Sidae Gunggwol Jangshik Giwa ui Giwon gwa Uimi." Master's thesis, Gukmin University, 2004.

Hong, Soon-min. "The management of royal palaces and the changes of 'the dual palace managing system' in Choson dynasty." Ph.D. diss., Seoul National University, 1996.

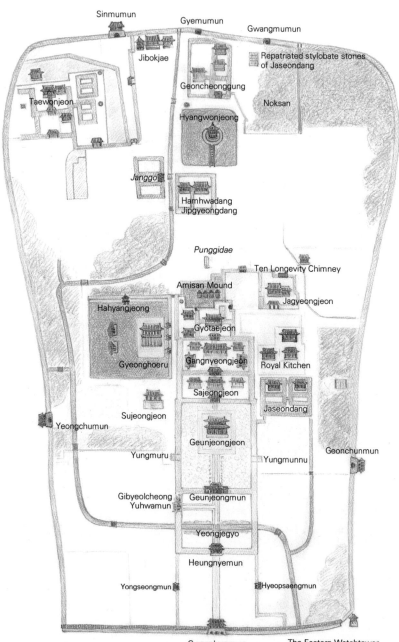

◉ The Map of Gyeongbokgung Palace

Sinmumun

Gyemumun

Gwangmumun

Jibokjae

Repatriated stylobate stones
of Jaseondang

Geoncheonggung

Noksan

Taewonjeon

Hyangwonjeong

Janggo

Hamhwadang
Jipgyeongdang

Punggidae

Ten Longevity Chimney

Amisan Mound

Jagyeongjeon

Hahyangjeong

Gyotaejeon

Gyeonghoeru

Gangnyeongjeon

Royal Kitchen

Sajeongjeon

Jaseondang

Sujeongjeon

Yeongchumun

Geunjeongjeon

Geonchunmun

Yungmuru

Yungmunnu

Gibyeolcheong
Yuhwamun

Geunjeongmun

Yeongjegyo

Heungnyemun

Yongseongmun

Hyeopsaengmun

Gwanghwamun

The Eastern Watchtower